The Productive Author's

GUIDE *TO*

DICTATION

SPEAK YOUR WAY TO HIGHER (AND HEALTHIER!) WORD COUNTS

Includes a Guided 24-day Program to Discover Which Dictation Practice Works Best for You

by

Cindy Grigg

Misch Masch
Publishing,
LLC

ISBN: 978-1-939582-23-2

PUBLISHER'S DISCLAIMER

THE PRODUCTIVE AUTHOR'S GUIDE TO WRITING
The Series

The Productive Author is an imprint for non-fiction guide books within Misch Masch Publishing. Works include other books in the *The Productive Author's Guide to Writing* series.

Each title is focused on timeless writing principles as applied to practical technology tools.

Find other titles by visiting TheProductiveAuthor.com.

Connect With Us on Social Media

Join our communities and get connected to all the deals and goings-on!

THE PRODUCTIVE AUTHOR:

Twitter:

http://www.twitter.com/ProductiveAuth

Facebook:

http://www.facebook.com/TheProductiveAuthor

Instagram:

http://www.instagram.com/ProductiveAuth

Pinterest:

http://www.pinterest.com/ProductiveAuth

SOCIAL LINKS FOR AUTHOR CINDY GRIGG:

Google+:

https://plus.google.com/+CindyGrigg/

Twitter:

https://twitter.com/Cindy_Grigg

Facebook:

https://www.facebook.com/authorcindygrigg

Goodreads:

http://www.goodreads.com/user/show/19382357-cindy

Instagram:

http://www.instagram.com/cindygrigg

LinkedIn:

http://www.linkedin.com/pub/cindy-grigg/56/4ba/7a9

Pinterest:

http://www.pinterest.com/CindyGrigg

Table of Contents

.

About the Author

Cindy Grigg has taught typing, transcription, and other office software and business productivity courses for nearly ten years at various educational institutions.

She is About.com's Expert of Office Software, writing about consumer technology and productivity.

Check out Office.About.com for free productivity resources for home, school, or professional projects.

She is also a speculative fiction author of science fiction and fantasy, including steampunk.

Check out CindyGrigg.com for press kit, blog, books, updates, and free resources for writers.

Who This Book is For

This book was written primarily for creative writers; however, learning to dictate can be relevant for non-fiction writers, stay-at-home parents, teachers, small business owners, restaurateurs, business moguls—you get the gist.

How much do you write? Would you rather speak it, assuming it didn't feel awkward?

Because it lengthens your leash. As in, that invisible tether that determines how long you have to stay fastened to a chair. Imagine being able to craft your words, worlds, and wild propositions for humanity to mull over, while having more freedom. Dictation is about a more flexible writing lifestyle.

Dictation can also manufacture more hours in the day-- or seems to, because dictation is potentially faster than typing or handwriting. As in, epically faster in my experience. This guide gives you an overview as well as a practical framework for what learning dictation is likely to require of you.

Those are two of the main reasons I've found for embracing dictation, but in the next few pages I'll introduce you to many more.

What This Book Isn't

Please know that *The Productive Author's Guide to Dictation* does not include specific buying advice for you individually. Like Economics 101 taught us, the tradeoffs among accuracy, price, and plenty of other factors can be widely different from person to person.

For that reason, I'm of course not going to tell you what you should buy or not buy and obviously some legwork and research of your own should be expected. I do make general recommendations and tell you what I use.

Please also know that this resource is not intended to replace full-fledged, program-specific how-to guides. Programs such as Dragon NaturallySpeaking now have interactive tutorials as soon as you start the program, not to mention 100+-page user manuals, quick start guides, and many other resources.

Finally, this book is not a magic wand because your own practice is required; it's a lever to make the required work easier.

But this book is still plenty of things...

What This Book Is!

The Productive Author's Guide to Dictation is the book I wish I'd had when I started adopting this skill.

In summary, this guide gives you an overview of available software and hardware for dictation, as well as a 4-week plan of drills for becoming more comfortable with dictation. These exploratory exercises go over major commands users of Nuance's Dragon software should focus on, both because it is the most popular dictation tool on the market and because it packs enough features to serve as a conceptual baseline for other programs you may opt for instead.

While focused on how to dictate fiction, this guide can be applied to non-fiction or academic writing as well.

More specifically, you get:

· *A 4-week (24-day), 3-stage system for mastering dictation skills while finishing 55,000 words in your work in progress, in about two hours per day! (estimated, each person's learning speed varies)*

· *26 dictation drills to mix and match according to what works best for you in three areas: General Commands, Verbal Storytelling, and Creative Flow*

· *Prompted and unprompted dictation passages from classic literature (from works of Bram Stoker, Charles Dickens, Jane Austen, James Joyce, Lewis Carroll, and others)*

· *Overviews of voice assistant, speech recognition, and transcription software options for Mac, Windows,*

Windows Phone, iOS, Android, and BlackBerry, including dozens of mobile apps

· *Overviews and comparison tables of transcription hardware accessories including digital recorders and external microphones or headsets*

· *Overviews of hiring and working with a human transcriptionist, should you decide to go that route instead*

· *Overviews and links to more information on dictation features within note-taking apps like Evernote, Microsoft OneNote, and Google Keep*

· *Tips for dictating web searches, email, word processed documents, spreadsheets, slide shows, notes, social media updates, and more*

· *Links to where you can find more in-depth guides and resources*

· *A stray pep talk or two (while learning dictation is absolutely worth it, you'll need them!)*

"I call people rich when they're able to meet the requirements of their imagination."

— Henry James,

The Portrait of a Lady

Introduction: Why I Wrote This Book

One of the first things to cross my mind as I began dictating my fiction writing was Gilbert and Sullivan's *Thoroughly Modern Millie*, a musical turned movie with Julie Andrews playing a thoroughly modern 1920s 'stenog'.

Stenographers typed out correspondence and other documents, often while their bosses like Millie's crush Trevor Grayson narrated the content to them.

Millie was interested in being on the cutting edge, or thoroughly modern. So were the many typists before her who used a typewriter. Most writers today would agree the word processor is a vast improvement.

So I pose this question to you: *What if there is a new tool as revolutionary to your writing process as the word processor was?*

Because dictation has so many advantages and can become such a life-changer for how you work, I created this book as a guide for you to investigate the full scope of tools available--and there are a bunch of 'thoroughly modern' options. After all, it's not 1925. It's not even 1975, 1995, or 2005.

Use what's available!

Or at least know what's out there so you can decide whether or not to leverage dictation toward your writing goals.

What is Dictation Software?

Dictation software is known by many names because solutions come in various forms with differing capabilities. They all have one thing in common: helping you leverage your voice toward getting your writing projects done.

In the next few pages, I'll introduce you to some of the terms you may run into as you get started. Keep in mind, this is one of those fields where terms may be used interchangeably and at times incorrectly. Focus on the concept of what a program does, so you can make sure those solutions you buy can do what you want them to.

Dictation Terms and Types to Know

Here's a quick orientation to a few terms and dictation tool types. Each can get much more technical, so please know these are simplified definitions, focused on what the end-user is trying to accomplish.

· **Transcription Software or Dictation Software:** A blanket term that can encompass all these other terms.

· **Digital Dictation:** Tools which allow a transcriptionist to more easily type recorded audio into digital text.

· **Digital Recorders:** Tools which record or edit audio in real-time.

· **Speech or Voice Recognition:** Tools which translate audio to digital text.

· **Speech-to-text:** Tools which translate audio to digital text.

· **Command and Control:** Tools that let you navigate an operating system and its programs or the web the way you might with a mouse or keyboard shortcuts.

· **Voice Assistant or Personal Assistant:** Similar to command and control solutions, but assistants offer contextual suggestions and typically speak back to you.

· **Remote Mics:** Tools (apps) that turn a mobile device into a microphone, so you are less tied to your desktop.

A Brief History of Dictation Tech

Dictation is just storytelling—and certainly so for fiction writers. All sorts of writers tell stories, however. Whether you write non-fiction, maintain a blog, or want to record your personal history or journal, dictation can help make your projects less dreamt and more done.

Consider that storytellers began by speaking, not writing, their words. Dictation can be thought of as going back to the fundamentals of human storytelling.

The first transcription machines were of course humans: disciples at the feet of religious leaders or philosophers, family members helping ailing authors, stenographers facilitating correspondence in business offices, and so on.

As for machines, there is some disagreement on who invented what when, but along the way it seems Thomas Edison invented the phonograph (1870s), followed by Alexander Graham Bell's invention of the graphophone (1920s), followed by the Philips Company's invention of recordable mini-cassettes (1960s), followed by the invention of digital dictation in the1980s. Today desktop software, mobile apps, and web-integrated solutions have brought even more options.

This means recording has made the diaphanous leap from being recorded in wax to being recorded in *the Cloud*, referring to the use of software housed on remote servers rather than on your own computing device, thanks to an internet connection. That's pretty amazing!

But the real question for you, the busy writer, is what point along that developmental continuum maximizes your writing experience and output. That perspective is partly what this book is for. Its other purpose is to equip you with a framework which allows you to learn to dictate—because, as mentioned, *that* can be a bit tricky. But so worth it!

Why I Invested Time to Learn Dictation

"The changes in our life must come from the impossibility to live otherwise than according to the demands of our conscience not from our mental resolution to try a new form of life."

— Leo Tolstoy

I began looking at dictation for several reasons. Like many people, I have experienced back problems, nerve problems, and a few scares with repetitive motion injuries. I've also had trouble with weight since becoming a full-time writer. All motivating reasons to find another way of doing things!

You might relate to these reasons or have some of your own, but my bet is that everyone who writes could benefit from dictation.

I learned for myself through trial and error. I'm not particularly adept at 'just doing things well' but I am pretty dedicated to the art of re-approach, once I'm motivated by enough advantages to something.

I wrote this book to capture all I learned in the hope that anyone who is interested in doing the same might be able to get to those advantages faster. Some things worked and others bottomed out. Once I cleared away the dross, I realized I had a collection of pretty interesting strategies toward breaking the dictation barrier. This is a combination of strategy and practice, with three levels of improvement.

As helpful as I hope my system is, though, I want to emphasize that you'll still need to put in your time with the practice. But at least you won't waste as much time as I initially did on ineffective dictation methods.

After all, this is all about getting your writing projects done!

For me the effort continues to pay off, which is why I'm such a nerd about it. Dictation has been a total game-changer. Since this is what I do for a living, it's been a life-changer.

9 Ways I've Used Dictation

While I do use the convenience of desktop dictation, where I sit in front of my laptop and speak as the dictation software 'types' the words for me, I tend to take more advantage of mobile dictation.

I use both the Dragon Mobile App for iOS (which requires an internet connection) and a digital dictation recorder (which requires batteries and which I have to then input into Dragon--more on how to do this in future sections).

You can utilize desktop and mobile dictation wherever you and society deem appropriate but here are ways I have used this technology, to spark your imagination:

1. The same way I did before, sitting in front of my desktop

While you can go mobile with dictation, you don't have to. As already mentioned, you can 'write' exactly the way you do now at your desk by speaking rather than typing your words. To that point, you can of course do a mix by dictating some things and typing others. Turning on a dictation program does not typically disable the keyboard.

2. While outlining

You can find dozens of ways to outline. Whether you use a word processor for a multilevel outline, a presentation program for storyboarding, or like me, a spreadsheet, you can get your ideas out more quickly. You can also use some Dragon dictation commands in specialty writing programs like Scrivener.

3. While researching

You can't exactly ramble aloud to yourself in every library space, for example, but you can rent out rooms and you can find remote corners in very large libraries. I found a space under some stairs in a nearby university library so that I could drag books down there and rattle off my findings as I read, rather than checking out the books and hauling them around. At home, I dictate ideas while watching documentaries. I simply pause the show and speak my notes into Dragon, then resume.

4. While doing social media or blogging

Many dictation programs let you update social media using voice commands. You can also whip out a blog post or email.

5. While preparing for conferences and presentations

While commands are more limited, you can dictate a presentation. I have used dictation to create Microsoft PowerPoint presentations for writing conferences.

6. While traveling abroad

I practiced with mobile recordings while traveling. I was able to describe inspiring places as I would to someone on the phone. I people-watched while I described what my fictional characters were thinking or doing. Being able to do so quickly allowed me to make the most of my limited time in the country.

7. While walking my own environs

I find dictating while walking to be most effective in natural, quieter settings. Think low-key park or woodsy walk, not busy city streets—though many tools claim to still work in noisy environments. I found that Dragon does alright in urban environments, for example, but I have a hard time thinking and staying alert to traffic.

8. While doing other 'mindless jobs'

The *very* first time I dictated was nearly a decade ago as I cleaned apartments of students who had left for the summer. That was a gritty business. So many grease-stained stove splashbacks. So many floors waxed. So many toilets. It was, however, incredible inspiration. As I cleaned I had so many writerly ideas popping and spoke them into a tape recorder which I then went home and typed. Now that's all so much easier thanks to dictation software doing the typing for me. I can capture my ideas while doing most housework—not that housework happens all that regularly at my place. But when it does, I often dictate my way through it.

9. While being more active within my office space

I find that physical activity helps me dictate. If it's stormy outside, I hold a plank, stretch, or ride my exercise bike while dictating. You might be able to do some of these things via desktop dictation, but it's of course simpler not to drag your laptop around the room. Obviously, drag your phone or digital recorder around instead!

13 Benefits of Dictation

Dictation has been readily utilized in legal, medical, automotive, financial, insurance, education, journalism, and government organizations for record keeping. You could ask, why are those people convinced about dictation? They'd likely tell you it saves them time, while allowing them to focus on the most efficacious aspects of their professional practice.

What writer doesn't want that?! Doesn't it make sense for all kinds of writers to at least consider this option? Especially since we tend to do *more writing* than these other professions!

Here is a list of 13 advantages to dictation:

1. Speed

Typing, I usually do about 900 words per hour. My dictation average, even with tons of pauses and slow speaking, is about 2,000-2,500 words an hour and many dictationists are faster than I am. If I do this for three hours, I average 7500 words. Sure, that's pure draft copy, but it's out there! For NaNoWriMo, you need about 1667 words a day for 30 days or closer to 2000 for 24 days to reach the 50,000-word goal.

Dictation should probably be seen as any NaNoWriMo-er's new best friend!

If you don't believe that you talk faster than you type, take an online typing quiz (or just type in Microsoft Word and check the lower left of the program interface for word count) then read the same thing out loud into an online dictation program like TalkTyper while you run a timer.

However, remember that *creating* text on the fly is always more difficult than just reading something.

2. Mobility

The ability to reduce butt-in-chair time is pretty much priceless. With desktop dictation software, you can set up desktop or remote mics such that you can roam all over the room or your entire house while babbling your masterpiece. With digital dictation recorders or dictation apps for your mobile phone, you can walk in the park or take a hike in the mountains while babbling your masterpiece. *Awesome!!*

"...and the great advantage of being a literary woman, was that you could go everywhere and do everything." —Henry James, The Portrait of a Lady

3. Multitasking

I don't readily believe in the efficiency of multitasking— but I have exceptions. Being able to complete a mental task like speaking a chapter in my novel while say, doing my planks, stretching, folding laundry, or other mindless tasks makes sense to me.

4. Focus

You can also use dictation to stay on task. You can't exactly check Twitter or BuzzFeed as easily mid-dictation. I've found that it requires more of my mind, thus creating more focus.

5. Spelling

Are you able to say words you could never spell? Dictation can smooth that over because the software is doing the spelling for you.

6. Prevention of Repetitive Motion Injuries

Constricting our hands, shoulders, neck, and spine in order to type can take its toll. Many writers are professionals working on computers by day. Add morning or night writes to the mix and you're increasing your likelihood of repetitive motion injuries like carpal tunnel or eye strain. Since writing is a long game, it really makes sense to be preventative.

7. External Inspiration

Dictation allows me to be 'on my way somewhere' while experiencing new muses and creative stimuli. Even if I'm just at home, I can refer to visual prompts more easily, such as a book about period fashions, for example.

8. Strengthened Storytelling Voice

As in, the tone with which you tell the story. Many authors write with a different voice than they speak with, and that may be the right choice at times, but more often your conversational tone tends to be a great voice to write in. Dictation brings out that conversational, authentic side of you.

9. Continuity and Flow

Because you are moving more quickly through the scene, emotion, or plot point, pacing can be improved. This is of course different for every writer, but my experience has been that dictation improves my storytelling continuity.

10. Reduced Internal Editor

Yes, you can edit in dictation programs, but many people draft more than they edit in dictation programs, and that's a good thing. It lets you create while holding your internal editor at bay. It's harder to stop and doubt yourself.

11. Increased Mental Dexterity

For me, dictating feels like you are creating from a different part of the brain. While initially frustrating, that's not necessarily a bad thing. I figure I'm also keeping my mind active by asking it to work in different ways.

12. A Leg Up On the Future

Dictation is a practical skill given emerging technologies, as evidenced by improved voice assistants on our phones, for example. Time invested in dictation should be valued as keenly relevant, just like learning to type better has been keenly relevant to most of us.

"Mastery of language affords one remarkable opportunities." — Alexandre Dumas

13. And Finally, What Cosmic Company You'll Keep

Dictation was the chosen form of many classic novelists. You have to ask, why have writers since abandoned it?

Check out these interesting stories about famous authors who used dictation:

Leo Tolstoy received one of the Dictaphone's earliest prototypes. To this he replied that the "Ediphone" was impressive but "too dreadfully exciting" for his methods. Instead, he seemed to favor dictating to his daughter Alexandra or even house guests.

Fyodor Dostoyevsky reportedly struck a bargain with his publisher to pay off his and/or his brother's debts. The deal required that the author turn in his manuscript for *The Gambler* in short order. To do so, he employed stenographer Anna Grigorievna, who gave him collaborative feedback as well. He finished the manuscript in four weeks then married Anna. The ultimate NaNoWriMo!

Thomas Hardy dictated his wife Florence Hardy's 'biography' about himself to her, seemingly to retain control of the account. Like many authors, Hardy also dictated once he became ill. Stricken with pleurisy, he spoke his last poem to his wife Florence.

John Milton was blind when he created *Paradise Lost,* dictating the epic poetical work to his several daughters. This inspired paintings of him and his daughters by artists George Romney, Delacroix, and others.

Alexander Dumas was rumored to never touch up his drafts, having served as a historian, which had given him practice in thinking about what he wanted to say before he dictated it.

Michel de Montaigne, an acclaimed 16th-century essayist, dictated his journal and possibly other writings.

Henry James referred to his hired transcriptionists as amanuenses, needing to contract such help at least partially due to rheumatism in his wrist. One of them, Theodora Bosanquet, recorded in her diary, "Indeed, at the time when I began to work for him, he had reached a stage at which the click of the Remington machine acted as a positive spur. He found it more difficult to compose to the music of any other make. During a fortnight when the Remington was out of order he dictated to an Oliver typewriter with evident discomfort, and he found it almost disconcerting to speak to something that made no responsive sound at all."

William Wordsworth was a kindred spirit to mobile writers such as myself. He 'wrote' *Tintern Abbey* mentally on a "ramble of four or five days...Not a line of it was altered, and not any part of it written down till I reached Bristol." Thanks to transcriptionist Isabella Fenwick, he also dictated *The Fenwick Notes* commentary about his poetry. Of his long poem *The Excursion,* Wordsworth mentions, "Something must now be said of this poem, but chiefly, as has been done through the whole of these notes, with reference to my personal friends, and especially to her who has perseveringly taken them down from my dictation."

Charles Dickens was rumored to act his characters out in front of a mirror, giving vocal dramatizations of dialogue and text. In 1882, *The Brooklyn Daily Eagle* published an interview with someone who claimed to be Dickens' amanuensis, describing him this way: "'Yes, I did shorthand work for Mr. Dickens for eighteen months. I did not take dictation for any of his novels, only his fugitive pieces...Most people seem to think Dickens was a ready writer. This is by no means the case. He used to come into his office in St. Catherine Street about eight o'clock in the morning and begin dictating. He would walk up and down the floor several times after dictating a sentence or a paragraph and ask me to read it. I would do so, and he would, in nine cases out of ten, order me to strike out certain words and insert others. He was generally tired out by eleven o'clock, and went down to his club on the Strand. A singular thing was that he never dictated the closing paragraphs of his story. He always finished it himself. I used to look in the paper for it, and find that he had changed it very greatly from what he had dictated to me. Dickens had a very odd habit of combing his hair. He would comb it a hundred times in a day. He seemed never to tire of it. The first thing he did on coming into the office was to comb his hair. I have seen him dictate a sentence or two, and then begin combing. When he got through he dictated another sentence."

Bram Stoker was himself a secretary and director of London's Lyceum Theatre, as well as a manager for Henry Irving. His own experiences may have influenced how several chapters of *Dracula* are dedicated to asylum director Dr. Seward recording dictations on a phonograph, to the chagrin of Mina Harker, who typed them up as soon as possible, believing the veracity and emotion of the audio to be too much for other readers to bear. "I have copied the words on my typewriter, and none other need now hear your heart beat, as I did." Dictation is also mentioned in Stoker's *The Jewel of Seven Stars*.

Stendhal (the pen name for Marie-Henri Beyle) dictated *The Charterhouse of Parma* in seven weeks, 52 consecutive days--another kindred spirit to all us NaNoWriMo's!

Marcel Proust dictated the *Death of Bergotte* to Celeste Albaret on his death bed, even though it was already finished, saying it needed to written a second time. He supposedly explained, "I didn't yet know what it's like to die when I wrote it. I know it more now."

James Joyce found inspiration in a random happening while dictating *Finnegan's Wake*. While recording the story, Joyce was interrupted when someone came to the door and was welcomed with a phrase like, "Come in," which Joyce thought worked well in the manuscript so he left it in.

Thomas Aquinas was apparently so skilled at dictation that he gave observers the impression he could speak on several topics at once to multiple scribes and even to dictate in his sleep.

Admittedly, this last point took me on a bit of a tangent, but it emphasizes the advantage of joining the ranks of some amazing authors. They were *kinda good at writing*, not to mention more modern dictationists like Kevin J. Anderson, Dan Brown, and Winston Churchill.

Think of how all these advantages could add value to you over the course of your productive life.

So don't fear the learning curve. Even though storytelling has been verbal for eons of time, that's not how we've been taught. We are programmed to feel efficient by sitting in a chair, moving our fingers across a keyboard configuration purposely designed to slow down our typing so that typewriter keys wouldn't jam into one another. Isn't that kooky? Deprogramming that mindset takes some work.

Speaking your story rather than typing or handwriting it *feels* less efficient at first, but even as you fumble it's as fast if not faster than typing or handwriting. As mentioned, I feel nearly every fiction or non-fiction writer could benefit from dictation. Keep in mind, you can still type when you want to, but dictation opens a whole new dimension.

Introduction to Dictation Software

As you start deciding among dictation tools, keep in mind that the game dictation developers are playing is to try to understand incredibly intricate speech nuances such as parsing, the ability for software to detect the difference between *that's tough* and *that stuff*, or *I scream* and *ice cream*, for example.

The software is not 100% accurate but it's pretty stinking good!

The over-arching thing to keep in mind is that the whole point of dictation software is maximizing accuracy and convenience, so it can be valuable to invest in the right tools. The rub is, each person's parameters for maximizing price and value are different, so some searching of your own is inevitable.

I've pared the beastly search down for you. What follows here is an overview of available tools for desktop, mobile, and web including those dictation tools already available on your device or computer or apps and programs you might already have, all with direct links for you to dive deeper according to your interests.

I am not affiliated or compensated by any of these developers or companies. Skim or devour as you see fit!

Note: In this section, you may see underlined links. These are clickable in the eBook version, but I've left them in this print version so you can have a search term to go by when searching online for additional information.

The Software You'll Probably End Up With: Dragon

Nuance offers many affordable products for different systems and price points. Here's a summary to get you oriented.

Please keep in mind that software packages change, so always refer to the manufacturer's site or representatives for current information. The following is intended to help you be acquainted with the software, but more recent versions may be available by the time you read this.

Keep in mind that for desktop, Dragon works in conjunction with tools you are already using, meaning, you will still be working in Microsoft Word, Corel WordPerfect, or even Scrivener, for example. You'll just have Dragon operating on your screen as well.

· Dragon NaturallySpeaking for PC Premium Edition (starting at about $199.99 USD)

· Dragon Dictate for Mac (about $199.99 USD)

· Dragon NaturallySpeaking Home Edition for Windows (about $99.99 USD)

· Dragon Dictation App for iOS (Free) – An app that transcripts your voice into text or commands

· Dragon Assistant (Free) – A personal assistant

· Dragon Go! (Free) – A mobile web search tool

· Dragon Remote Mic App (Free) – Turns your iOS or Android phone into a mobile microphone

Most writers will opt for the desktop version, either Home or Premium.

I chose Premium over the Home version because it offers Bluetooth wireless dictation options beyond the Wireless Remote Mic App, better ability to playback my portable digital recorder (so Dragon NaturallySpeaking transcribes it into my Microsoft Word document), audio file conversion, more options for customizing commands, more options for inserting ubiquitous text and graphics, and more dictation possibilities in spreadsheets and presentations. Premium can be a budget-stretcher, but it's good value for the money.

For about $100 USD more, you can also get a Wireless version of Dragon which includes a wireless microphone headset, or a Mobile version which includes a digital recorder. My two cents is to opt for the regular versions and buy those accessories separately. Doing so just gives you maximum control.

While you can get previous versions of Dragon for a discount, I suggest jumping into Dragon 13 (released Fall 2014) for desktop because I like a lot of its new features:

· Up to a 20% improvement in out-of-the-box accuracy (not exactly new as this is compared to version 11, but still)

· Dragon 13 can be taught to recognize your voice with more accuracy if you grant it permission to learn from your Sent email (in Gmail or Yahoo Mail)

· Searchable Vocabulary Editor with new features including custom dictation commands

· Web experience – Full Text Control in most websites while using Chrome, Firefox, and Internet Explorer

· Improved Learning Center (called Dragon Sidebar in previous versions), Help Center, and Interactive Tutorial

· The New DragonBar (hoovers above your other applications making it easy to switch dictation on or off), with more customization such as collapsing or moving the bar. If you like Dragon 12's bar better, you can opt for it instead.

Nuance also offers pricier professional versions and several additional products. For further comparison, check out Nunace's Dragon NaturallySpeaking Feature Matrix and Nuance's Dragon Deals Site.

Dictation Software and Apps for Desktop Computers

Even though some of what we do in a given day has moved to mobile devices like smartphones or tablets, desktop computers and laptops are still the productivity powerhouses among most writers I know.

This section focuses on Windows and Mac. Linux users should be able to find solutions as well by searching online.

The next few pages go over dictation tools already likely to be on your computer as well as third-party tools like Dragon to take those capabilities to the next level.

Built-in Dictation on Windows

Windows Speech Recognition allows you to control your computer and create documents on your Windows desktop using your voice. That means you need to both train the system to better recognize your voice as well as learn the dictation conventions and commands.

This section does not seek to replicate that training and documentation you can find on Microsoft's site: Dictation on Windows 7 and Dictation on Windows 8.

This overview is meant to make you aware that your computer may already have speech recognition capabilities you are not using, and to help you decide whether this is enough power for you, or whether you want something like Dragon.

Preparation

· Use your computer's internal mic or improve accuracy by connecting a microphone to your computer.

· Complete any setup prompts you are instructed to. This helps you create a voice profile by allowing the system to learn your voice patterns.

· Learn commands (similar to mouse or keyboard commands but with your voice) to tell the computer what to do.

How to Start Speech Recognition

Want to just give it a whirl? After all, it is free with Windows 7 or 8. Search your computer for 'Speech Recognition' or select Start – All Programs – Accessories – Ease of Access – Windows Speech Recognition. Or, on Windows 8, search for Windows Speech Recognition.

Online Resources (search by the following article titles):

· Common Commands in Windows Speech Recognition

· Microsoft Accessibility Support

Built-in Dictation on Mac

Traditionally, Apple's Dictation for Mac allowed you to type but not to control your computer on desktop computers running OS X Mountain Lion or later. Commands were available as 'speakable items'.

In speech recognition for OS X Yosemite, these have been merged and over 50 editing and formatting commands have been added to Dictation.

Preparation

Your version of Dictation may only work for 30 seconds at a time and require an internet connection. You'll therefore want to be sure to check out Enhanced Dictation. When this is activated, you dictate in an ongoing fashion that does not require an internet connection though it may require additional initial downloads from the internet (large at about 800 MB).

Find full training, documentation, and official system requirements here: Dictation on Mac.

How to Activate Dictation

Want to just jump in. It's free! Select Apple – System Preferences – View – Dictation & Speech – On.

Or, from within an application select anywhere you would normally type then select Edit – Start Dictation or press the Function key twice (fn), pressing this again to end the dictation.

How to Activate Enhanced Dictation

Set this up by selecting Apple – System Preferences – Dictation & Speech – Enable Enhanced Dictation.

Resources (remember, you can search for these articles online):

· OS X Mountain Lion: Use spoken commands to control your Mac

· OS X Mavericks: Use spoken commands to control your Mac

· OS X Yosemite: Dictate your messages and documents

More Dictation Options for Desktops

In addition to Dragon, here are a few more software options for desktop:

- Tazti ($29.99 USD) – Windows - by Voice Tech Group, Inc. This is speech recognition software that can also be used to command your computer or video games. You can also create up to 300 custom speech commands then archive or transfer them.

- VoxCommando – This speech recognition program can work with multimedia programs like XBMC and iTunes. Its accuracy is enhanced by accessing the media in your libraries, behind the scenes. Great for commanding home setups, like you're captain of the Enterprise.

- If you're still stuck in the dark ages, consider DeskBot for older versions of Windows.

Not enough Mac options? Users may be able to run Windows programs via desktop virtualization software such as Parallels.

Open Source Speech Recognition Resources

As for open source resources, check out CMU (Carnegie Melon University) Sphinx for desktop and PocketSphinx for mobile. As a user, you can benefit open source development efforts by submitting your voice data.

One way to do this is to consider being a reader for LibriVox, a community where volunteers read to create free audiobooks. Those recordings can then be submitted to VoxForge.

Practicing reading aloud will also give a little boost to your dictation efforts—you'll be more practiced in speaking a story.

As for open source suites, OpenOffice reportedly works better with Dragon than LibreOffice but neither responds to all commands. I would like to look at specific differences more in the future but my current assessment is that both performed similarly and both utilized Dragon's Dictation Box feature, a dialog box that creates an environment you can dictate in. Similarly, I was able to use Dragon with Microsoft Office Online through the Dictation Box feature. Most other software for Windows should be the same in this regard.

Dictation Software and Apps for Mobile Devices

Mobile dictation software and apps are effective but streamlined. These will not have nearly the same features available as full desktop versions. For example, Dragon's mobile app for iOS is considered a companion app to the desktop versions.

Additionally, the few true transcription apps available on the market typically require an internet connection because the transcription is actually taking place on a remote server, in the cloud, then sent back to your device. Many solutions listed here are merely recording apps. You would then contract with a service to transcribe the audio or attempt to have software listen to your digital recording (this can get sketchy—consider a digital recorder rather than your smartphone for this).

In the next few pages, I'll also explain the basics about voice assistants you may or may not already use on your mobile device (Android, iOS, Windows Phone, and BlackBerry).

6 Tips for Dictating to a Mobile Device

1. **Be secure.** While convenient, dictating to the cloud or the web can pose security issues. Be sure your device and connection are protected.

2. **Get a great connection.** Your best accuracy will come with better internet connections, so relying on unpredictable signals is not advised.

3. **Talk into the microphone**. This implies knowing where the microphone is on your device. For example, your iPhone may have microphones at the bottom while your iPad has one at the top.

4. **Seek quiet but also experiment with noise.** While the quieter your dictation environment is the better, don't assume your mobile device can't handle some background noise. Your iPhone, for example, likely has a noise-canceling microphone for filtering out noise.

5. **You might benefit from accessories.** Mics and headsets are not just for desktop setups. Know that some external microphones may work with your phone or digital recorder, but others create a very faint recording due to the combined incoming and outgoing signals, for example. Always test a mic before dictating something lengthy. Experiment with how closely you hold the mic to your mouth.

6. **Don't say too much without looking at your screen:** With mobile dictation, your voice is typically sent to a remote server, so keep your eye on your mobile device now and then to see if it ever stops recording what you are saying.

Built-in Voice Assistant on Android: Google Now

Google Now is a mobile speech recognition and personal assistant utility for Android devices. It allows you to dictate in any place you typically type or key in text. Google Now is also available for iOS and desktop.

This means you can dictate web searches, emails, texts, and more.

How to Activate Google Now on Your Android Device

Turn Google Now on or off through the Google App. In this app, select Menu - Settings – Toggle On or Off for Google Now.

Special Features and Limitations to Know About

Google Now features cards, or panes of information intended to be front and center when you need them. The weather card, for example, was default on my Android device. Others include game highlights, traffic reports, nearby attractions, reminder notifications, boarding passes, physical activity trackers, and much more.

Check out Google Now's Landing Site. Also, I'll be going over the note-taking aspects of Google Now in an upcoming section.

More Voice Apps for Android

Here are some transcription, voice assistant, and recorder apps you may want to consider for Android devices.

Here are some transcription, voice assistant, and recorder apps you may want to consider for Android devices.

· Dragon Mobile Assistant by Nuance (Free) – Use this app to command your phone with your voice, including social media updates, text messages, and email as well as setting reminders, checking weather, and more. You can opt for an Attentive Mode which allows you to wake the app with your voice (no one else should be able to). Multiple response voices to choose from.

· Dragon Remote Microphone by Nuance (Free) – This app connects your desktop version of Dragon NaturallySpeaking over a WiFi network, freeing you up to roam a bit from your desktop.

· Speech to Text Translator by FSM Software (Free / $1.99 USD) – This is a 3-in 1 app including speech recognition, text to speech (TTS), and translator functions. Share your notes via email, SMS, social media, instant messaging (WhatsApp, Viber, Skype and more). Great for students, travelers, and business road warriors, for example. Purchase of the Speech to Text Unlocker for $1.99 USD gets rid of ads.

· Andy (Siri for Android) by 74tech.com (Free) – Another voice-controlled mobile assistant app. Features include: answers to general questions, launching other apps (including internet browsing), calendar, location and mapping services, math functions and currency conversions, email, making calls, music controls, photo searches, alarms, reminders, spelling words, and more.

·Jeanne (Siri for Android) by Pannous (Free) – Touts advanced Voice Search. Other features include, asking questions, voice dialing (contacts), sending emails, setting alarms and reminders, listening to music automatically and more.

·Skyvi – Siri for Android (Free / In-app purchases) by BlueTornado – Another voice controlled mobile assistant. Features include: answers to general questions, texting, directions, making calls, local weather, music controls and updating social media such as Facebook or Twitter. Skyvi can also tell you jokes. Disclaimer: Skyvi is not affiliated with Apple or Siri in anyway.

·Dictadroid Voice Recorder by SoftEight (Free / $2.99 USD) – A recording app. Share your recordings by email, MMS, FTP, Box, Google Drive, or Dropbox. For additional cost, the developers suggest Quicktate, a service that dictates your recordings and emails them back to you. Features include pause during recording and playback, inserting or overwriting in existing recordings, Automatic Voice Activity Detection, Audio Gain Control, recording when the screen isn't on, assigning photos to a recording, and more.

·Cogi – Notes and Voice Recorder by Cogi (Free / Premium available) – This is so interesting. Tap once for Cogi to begin listening. If you are in a lecture, for example, tap the screen when something interesting is said. The last 5 to 45 seconds of audio will be kept along with the recording, which you can stop with another tap. The idea is to only record the most compelling stuff.

·Hi-Q MP3 Voice Recorder by Yuku (Free / $3.99 USD) – A mobile sound recorder app with impressive reviews, featuring high-fidelity 44 kHz audio sampling, capture of real-time MP3 clips, front or back mic preferences, customizable input gain settings (for recording in different environments), and more. Share to Skype, WhatsApp, SoundCloud or store online with Dropbox, Evernote, Google Drive, and many others. Does not record calls.

· Easy Voice Recorderby Digipom (Free / $3.99 USD) – Another recording app. Features include recording in the background, save to an SD card, save recordings as a ringtone, record to various formats to save space, record in stereo, change input volume with microphone software gain, skip silent sections, switch to video microphone, record to a Bluetooth mic, and more. Does not record calls on most phones.

· Skyro Voice Recorder by Triveous (Free / $1 USD) – Sync your notes to a cloud service such as Dropbox with this app. Features include adjustable sample rate 8-44 kHz, file compression, geo-tagging, autosave, storage to an SD card, user interface themes, sharing to Soundcloud or via Bluetooth to Whatsapp, Evernote, Skype, Google Drive and more, record from the lock screen, and more.

· Tape-a-talk by Markus Drösser (Free / $1.32 USD) – A recorder app. Features include the ability to record voice when display is not on. The free version is called Tape-a-Talk Voice Recorder.

· RecForge II by Dje073 (Free / $3.99 Pro) is a recorder app. You may find the Lite version frustrating because it pauses recordings every 3 minutes, requiring you to unpause it to continue. Features include recording or converting files to mp3, ogg and wav formats as well as scheduled recordings, one-tap home screen widgets, skippable silence, audio editing, opting out of notifications (for more discretion), customizable gain, adjustable playback speed, mono or stereo, and more. Share recordings to Google Drive, DropBox, Box, social networks, mail, Bluetooth, and more.

· Speaktoit Assistant by Speaktoit (Free with in-app purchases) – The much-acclaimed Assistant can be used cross-platform (smartphone, tablet, or laptop). A customizable avatar helps by answering questions, executing voice commands, announcing events, connecting to the right web services or sites, call numbers and contacts, send and receive texts, send and receive email, use alarms, direction and location services, read the news, get weather, play music and video, translate, and much more. The developers claim you do not need to learn commands and makes recommendations depending on your time, place, and past requests, plus it can give proactive suggestions. You can also create new commands. Integrate with Google, Twitter, Facebook, Foursquare, Evernote, Yelp, TripAdvisor, Wikipedia, Chacha, IMDB, Eventful, News360, Amazon, Gmail, Google Images, Google Calendar, Google Maps, Google Navigation, Waze and more.

You can find tons of other apps as well, but the ones I have listed above are where I would start if I hadn't already decided on a combination of Dragon Mobile for iOS and the personal assistant utilities that come free with my devices.

Built-in Voice Assistant on iOS: Siri

Siri is a mobile speech recognition and personal assistant utility for iOS devices such as iPad, iPhone, and iPod Touch. It allows you to dictate in any field where you type or key in text.

This means you can dictate web searches, emails, texts, and more.

How to Activate Siri on Your iOS Device

Make sure Siri is turned on by selecting Settings – General – Siri. Then, a small microphone should appear next to your iOS on-screen keyboard, indicating that it is possible to dictate.

Tap the microphone icon, dictate your text, then select Done.

Features and Limitations to Know About

You can dictate punctuation, symbols, capitalization, returns or new paragraphs, new lines, and emoticons. These commands can vary based on your language preference so check here for full detail on how to speak these elements: Check Out Apple's Siri Site.

More Voice Apps for iOS

Here are more transcription, voice assistant, and recorder apps you may want to consider for iOS devices, the crown jewel being Dragon Mobile, in my opinion.

· Dragon Mobile Dictation for iOS by Nuance (Free) – This is the mobile app powered by Dragon NaturallySpeaking. Update social networking to Facebook and Twitter, see and send text or email messages, capture notes, and draft text for documents.

· PaperPort Notes for iPad by Nuance (Free) – This app lets you create one document out of other documents, audio, handwritten notes, typed notes, photographed or scanned documents turned to editable text, and web research, by integrating Dragon voice recognition. Includes markup for annotating notes and integration with popular cloud storage accounts.

· Google by Google, Inc. (Free) – This app includes many personal assistant features including Google Now cards.

· Cogi – Notes and Voice Recorder by Cogi (Free) – This is so interesting. Tap once for Cogi to begin listening. If you are in a lecture, for example, tap the screen when something interesting is said. The last 5 to 45 seconds of audio will be kept along with the recording, which you can stop with another tap. The idea is to only record the most compelling stuff.

· Audio Memos by Imesart S.a.r.l. ($0.99 USD) – This is an effective audio recorder. To make it more useful some in-app extensions should be purchased: Voice activated recording (to avoid pauses or silence), append audio to existing recordings, and send recordings to a computer using WiFi. Otherwise, you can upload to Dropbox, Google Drive, Box, Evernote, FTP or WebDAV.

· Recorder by Retronymns ($0.99 USD) – Features include recording, playback (including pause), search, WiFi syncing among devices (account required), visual track trimming, call recording (outbound), and more.

· Philips Dictation Recorder for iPhone by Speech Processing Solutions GmbH (Free) – A professional dictation and recorder app. Features include record, playback, insert new recording into initial recording track, overwriting, appending, settings for prioritizing recordings, file and app encryption, and more. Philips SpeechLive integrates the app with the cloud for more versatility. SpeechScribe immediate transcription service may cost more.

· iRecorder Pro by SIMPLETOUCH ($2.99 USD) – A recorder with WiFi transfer. Share files with iTunes. Features include adjustable playback speed for some iOS devices, pause during recording and playback, and the possibility of recording while iPhone is in sleep mode. No time limit to recordings and if the file is hefty SmartSplit helps you transfer it.

· Express Dictate Voice Dictation Software by NCH Software (Free) – A voice recorder and app for iPhone. Intended use is for Express Dictate files to be sent to a typist. Features are simplified "to closely mimic that of old style dictation recorders." Playback, rewind, insert or overwrite recordings, optional voice activated recording to eliminate dead space, and more.

You can find other apps as well, but the ones I have listed above are where I would start if I hadn't already decided on a combination of Dragon Mobile (iOS) and personal assistant utilities that come free with my devices.

Built-in Voice Assistant on Windows Phone: Cortana

Windows Phone Speech Recognition is a mobile dictation and personal assistant utility for Windows Phone smartphones and tablets. It allows you to dictate in any place you type or key in text.

This means you can dictate web searches, emails, texts, notes, and more.

How to Use Cortana on Your Windows Phone Device

...if it's available yet for your device. Hold down the Start button on your device. This turns dictation on for the future.

If you want to turn this on or off manually, select Settings - Speech - Toggle on or off for Enable Speech Recognition Service.

Features and Limitations to Know About

Cortana seeks to suggest things to you according to history and context. It's a powerful personal assistant. Check out Microsoft's Cortana site.

More Voice Apps for Windows Phone

Here are more transcription, voice assistant, and recorder apps you may want to consider for Windows Phone devices.

· Dictation Station by Bill DeNapps LLC (Free) – Speak your messages, emails, documents, blog posts, social media, notes, and more. Pin to-do lists. The app offers 'advanced punctuation commands' for more professional needs.

· DigiDictate Mobile by DigiDictate-Mobile (Free) This app allows you to access server-based data, meaning you can get to it anytime and anywhere. Touch-screen optimized with a recording interface "mimicking the slide-switch recording system".

· SpeechTrans Dictation by SpeechTrans, Inc. ($1.29 USD) – A cloud-centric app that lets you send to Microsoft OneNote, social media, email, phones, devices, and more. You can also link this to your Microsoft Account.

· Dictate! by BrilliSoft, LLC ($1.49 USD) - Use this app for speaking your text messages, emails, Microsoft Word documents, Facebook posts, notes, and more. The developers claim you can also use this in most other apps.

· Milkman by Matt McCormick (Free) – Milkman is a
mobile app that syncs to the popular online task tool
Remember The Milk. Set reminders and create or
update to-do lists. You can also set location-based
reminders and view lists in Live Tiles (home screen).
This app is not endorsed by Remember The Milk.

· Note+ by Aälejandro Díazs ($1.49 USD) - Capture
notes via dictation, then share or pin them to the
Start screen, OneDrive, and more. Minimal but
includes security features and automatic backup.

· Audio Notes by MAC, LLC ($0.99 USD) – This app
features one-touch recording, play, stop, and save.
Other features include recording notes and lists,
appending records, and resuming recording if
interrupted by another function.

You can find tons of other apps as well, but the ones I
have listed above are where I would start if I hadn't
already decided on a combination of Dragon Mobile
for iOS and the personal assistant utilities that come
free with my devices.

Built-in Voice Assistant on BlackBerry: BlackBerry Assistant

BlackBerry now has a voice assistant called BlackBerry Assistant. This is a contextual assistant that aims to follow what you do (speak to it, it speaks back; type to it, it types back, etc).

How to Begin Using BlackBerry Assistant

Tap the microphone icon to talk.

You can make sure BlackBerry Assistant is active (assuming it is on your device, which it may not be) by looking under Settings on your phone.

Features and Limitations to Know About

BlackBerry Assistant is also compatible with BlackBerry Messenger (BBM).

Your BlackBerry device may or may not have this available. It is still fairly new and was first available on the Passport.

Get more detail by visiting this BlackBerry blog post.

More Voice Apps for BlackBerry

Here are more transcription, voice assistant, and recorder apps you may want to consider for Android devices.

· DriveSafely Pro by iSpeech.org ($19.99 USD) - The goal of this app is to prevent distracted driving. It's a voice commanded mobile assistant app. It reads your texts and emails to you and allows you to reply or send with your voice. Make calls with just your voice. Choose whether messages play automatically or on-demand. Auto-response available.

· iSpeech Dictation by iSpeech.org (Free) - A more streamlined option from the makers of DriveSafely Pro. Speak texts, BlackBerry Messenger (BBM), email, and voice notes.

· Dictation Blue by Grundig Business Systems GmbH ($9.99 USD) – A recording and dictation app that works via Bluetooth to send your dictations to your email. Record, edit, and more. The automatic return feature is interesting. If your transcriptionist uses DigtaSoft, you can automatically import to that.

· Parrot - Voice Recorder by Searing Media Inc. (Free) – A recorder with sharing capabilities. With minimal taps you can capture, play, or share recordings to BBM, Text Message, Email, Bluetooth, NFC, BlackBerry Remember and more! The Pro version is not free but allows you to record your mobile calls (automatically or when asked). Pro also offers password protection, file attachments, an option to record to an SD card, track sorting, and handling of externally-captured recordings.

·Vlingo - Virtual Assistant by Vlingo Corporation (Free) – A voice controlled mobile assistant app. Location services, general questions, texting, social media updates. Check out the link for some pretty awesome endorsements including one from MC Hammer.

·VoicePro Transcriber by KeyStroke Pro ("Free") – A dictation and recording app. Record from your phone or send recordings to Keystroke Pro from anywhere. The app is free, but the transcription isn't. "You no longer have to use a computer and internet connection to send your dictations you simply click the upload button." Record, edit, append, play, and much more. No overall storage limits.

You can find tons of other apps as well, but the ones I have listed above are where I would start if I hadn't already decided on a combination of Dragon Mobile for iOS and the personal assistant utilities that come free with my devices.

More Dictation Alternatives

Call-in Dictation Services

While not as popular as some of these other mobile methods, call-in dictation systems let you dictate over the phone, just like it sounds. You place a call, enter a pin, and start dictating. You even might have controls such as pausing and playback. You then have an option to send the audio file where you would like.

Not the way I would go, but interesting.

One example is DictaSmart.

Online Dictation Tools

Most browsers do not innately offer dictation or speech recognition capabilities. You can, however, find a few sites to use online. As with mobile, be conscious of security as well as whether you maintain a good connection. You don't want to lose your work!

Checking out a free online speech to text tool is also a great way to try the drills in this book before deciding to invest in a desktop solution such as Dragon. Here are a few:

· Speechpad.pw (Free) Just go to this website, read the brief instructions and start dictating using many of the commands for Dragon. Some limitations of course, but a great simple tool. You may have to allow the program to access your device's microphone.

· TalkTyper (Free) Another awesome, simple speech recognition tool within your browser with a few more bells and whistles than Speechpad, including integration with Google Translate.

· Google Voice Search (Free) Use this to voice search and more in Chrome. Available in many languages.

· WebDictate (pricing varies) This web-based dictation download bills itself as ideal for organizations.

· VoiceBase, Inc.'s VoiceBase.com (pricing varies) Another solution for organizations, this web tool offers plenty of transcription and indexing features, including possible integration with Evernote. Your audio and video content is transcribed and made searchable.

Dictation in Popular Note-taking Programs

It makes sense to also investigate note-taking programs and apps. Maybe you didn't know a note-taking program you already use has audio recording capabilities, including transcription to digital text.

Or, maybe it will convince you to learn more about note-taking programs for mobile, web, or desktop.

If you have not already, check out three popular note-taking apps in the next few pages: Microsoft OneNote, Evernote, and Google Keep.

Dictation in Microsoft OneNote

Microsoft OneNote is a note-taking program available in three forms.

Where to Download Microsoft OneNote

· OneNote 2013 for desktop PC (free) or OneNote for desktop Mac (free) – The full-featured application bundled with many Microsoft Office suites can now also be installed for free on your Windows or Mac desktop.

· OneNote Online (OneNote.com) (free) – A streamlined version accessed through an internet site you log into

· OneNote Mobile (OneNote for Android, OneNote for Windows Phone, OneNote for iPhone) (free) – Streamlined versions of OneNote installed on your smartphone

· OneNote for iPad (free for limited features, subscription for more features) – Tablet version with mid-range functionality (more than for mobile but less than the desktop versions)

Dictaton Features to Know About

As About.com's Expert of Office Software, I offer a bunch of free online resources covering what you can do with OneNote, including some visual slide shows of tips and tricks. Check it out here:

Complete Guide to Microsoft OneNote: Quick Tips, Tricks, & How-to's

Dictation in Evernote

Evernote is another popular note-taking program you've likely heard about. It comes in a few different versions.

Where to Download Evernote

You can download Evernote for free across many operating systems.

· Evernote for Windows

· Evernote for Mac OS X

· Evernote - Android Apps on Google Play

· Evernote on the App Store on iTunes - Apple

More versions are available for a subscription fee. Evernote Premium(starting at $5/month for more features – I suggest this if you can afford it) and Evernote Business ($10/user/month).

Dictation Features to Know About

As About.com's Expert of Office Software, I offer a bunch of free online resources covering what you can do with Evernote, including some visual slide shows of tips and tricks. Check it out here:

Complete Guide to Evernote: Quick Tips, Tricks, & How-to's

Dictation in Google Keep

For a streamlined, online or Android version of a note-taking program, check out Google's web app Keep.

Where to Download Google Keep

All of the following are free ways to use Google Keep:

· Google Keep - Chrome Web Store

· Google Keep - Android Apps on Google Play

· For the web version – Login to your Google account – Select the 9-square Apps button in the upper right – More Apps – Keep. Or, go to:Keep.Google.com and login.

Google Keep Features to Know About

As About.com's Expert of Office Software, I offer a bunch of free online resources covering what you can do with Google Keep, including some visual slide shows of tips and tricks. Check it out here:

Complete Guide to Google Keep: Quick Tips, Tricks, & How-to's

Introduction to Dictation Hardware

Apart from your own computer or mobile device, which are way beyond the scope of this book, here is a quick overview of some dictation-related accessories you will want to consider.

You may have a bit of cash to invest in some nice dictation hardware or accessories but my guess is that your writerly budget has finite limits. Here's a quick overview and some affordable options so you can shop smarter.

Portable Digital Recorders

If you're taking your writing show on the road literally—and I think you should! It's totally liberating—you'll want to know about a few different types of hardware for capturing your voice.

Here's a quick overview followed by reviews of popular recorders.

· **Digital Dictation Recorders:** Typically handheld and battery-powered, these are portable devices used to record audio to WMA, WAV, MP3, DSS, and DS2 format extensions. The recordings are than sent to a human transcriptionist who types it out, upload for conversion by dictation software such as some versions of Dragon, or played aloud into a desktop or online version of dictation software.

· **Tape, Cassette or Microcasette Recorders**: A bit larger and more old-school than digital dictation, these are typically handheld and battery-powered portable devices that record to a physical cassette. The recording is than sent to a human transcriptionist who types it out or played aloud into a desktop version of a dictation software.

· **Mobile Phone App Recorders:** We already went over a bunch of these in the Dictating to Mobile sections of this guide, so this is just a reminder. With mobile dictation apps, one can record, edit, and send dictation files over networks. Some but not all require an internet connection. Aside from those, you can find apps that function offline as recorders.

My Two Cents: How Digital Trumps Cassette Tape Recording for Dictation

Some users are adamant about sticking with cassettes or microcassettes and I can sympathize with that. I still listen to audiocassettes in my kitchen because I'm a creature of nostalgia.

But here are some advantages to digital dictation:

1. Depending on the program, you can insert new audio content at random access points.

2. You can find and search audio files more easily.

3. You have the option to send your file to multiple typists which can be helpful for reducing errors or expediting a project by having different typists type different sections.

4. Backup! You have something to go back to even if the dictation software does something kooky and digital files make it easier to keep a backup in multiple places.

As ever, the bottom line is, do what works for you!

Comparison Chart of Affordable Digital Recorders

If you are interested in portable digital dictation devices, here are several to start your search with, followed by my personal choice and recommendation.

Bear in mind, much more expensive dictation devices are available and are often marketed to doctors, lawyers, podcasters and other professionals who want professional-grade audio.

I've stuck with those digital recorders writers are most likely to afford.

	Estimated Price	File Types	Capacity	Recording Time in Hours	Battery Life in Hours	Weight in Ounces
Olympus DM	$110 USD	MP3, WMA, PCM	4GB	1,000	50	3
Olympus WS	$120 USD	MP3, WMA, WAV	16GB	2,040	27	1.8
Philips DVT (or similar model)	$130 USD	MP3, WAV, MPEG	4GB	1140	48	2.1
Sony ICD-UX	$85 USD	MP3, AAC, WMA, WAV	4GB	1,070	30	2.6
Sony ICD-PX	$100 USD	MP3	4GB	1,070	96	2.1
Sony ICD-SX	$200 USD	MP3, WMA	16GB	630	19	2.6
Yamaha Pocketrak PR	$150 USD	MP3, WAV	2GB	50	30	3

I personally use the mid-range Sony from this list, the Sony ICD-PX. I chose it based on recording capacity, battery life, dimensions and price. It works superbly for me. I'm able to dictate on the go then upload it to my desktop version of Dragon NaturallySpeaking, as described in the next few pages.

Ways I've Downloaded or Converted Digital Recordings to a Desktop Dictation Program

I'm able to dictate while I'm out and about by recording tracks on my handheld digital recorder (I use a headset mic sometimes).

At home, I connect my digital recorder to my laptop and download all the audio files I created. I then open Dragon and select Tools – Transcribe Recording.

This method, however, did not work for me initially. I have not been able to concretely pinpoint why my first attempts at having Dragon transcribe a file resulted in poor accuracy, but for my first several months of dictating, I instead plopped the digital recorder in front of my laptop and pressed play so it could dictate to Dragon (I did have to play with volume on the recorder and distance from my laptop mic).

Now that I've revisited the Transcribe Recording option, I have seen better accuracy. Here are two considerations:

- After selecting Tools – Transcribe Recording, I selected the option to include Only Dictation Commands, which I believe helped improve Dragon's results for my dictations.

- Also, I found that accuracy was improved by setting up a second user profile (Profile – New User Profile).

If you do decide to play your audio recordings into Dragon while it takes the dictation, here are a few suggestions because it can be quirky:

· If using the playback method, place the digital recorder in different spacing from your computer, but I found the most luck by propping it upright just in front of my keyboard, with my laptop screen at 90 degrees (important because the mic is a small hole located on my laptop's screen). Also play with volume on the digital recorder. My accuracy was atrocious at 15 but awesome at 25, for example. Also, note that your laptop or computer's internal mic may be different than that of my mid-range Toshiba laptop bought earlier this year. Just know that results may vary and some shopping around and trial and error might be part of this process.

· While out and about, I found it helped for me to speak slightly louder when cars passed.

· For some reason, my setup could handle cars passing but never rivers. Go figure!

· When playing the recorded audio, be sure to check every 15 minutes or so if you can, to make sure your computer doesn't time out. You may have to play with settings so it does not go to sleep.

· The first few times you do this, you may see 'low quality' warnings pop up. I found it helpful to check the box for never showing these messages again. That way, my dictations were not interrupted by this message every time I tried to play my audio recordings into my desktop transcription software. Another option is to setup an additional user voice profile under Profile – New User Profile.

You also may be able to do a line-out connection from your digital recorder directly into your computer, which may help with accuracy.

It's all about finding those settings and methods that give you the greatest accuracy. When working on your dictation setup, keep your receipts and shop where you find great return policies!

Microphones and Headsets

Dictation is all about your voice input, so considering an external microphone beyond the built-in microphone in your computer or device makes sense. If you find you are not satisfied with the accuracy and results of your dictations, look into a few of these wired, wireless, or wearable mics, including desktop and headset versions.

Keep in mind, mics can become a useful tool for writers beyond transcription. It might be worthwhile to invest in an awesome tool. You may find it helpful for creating podcasts, collaborating with others over the internet, and other situations.

While the following sections are by no means a complete guide for selecting audio components (that could be an entire book itself), here are considerations that helped me choose a dictation microphone.

Additionally, one place for those looking at Dragon NaturallySpeaking for desktop is to check Nuance's Hardware Compatibility Sites. These can help you know whether a peripheral even has a shot of working with the software:

· Nuance-approved Microphones for Windows

· Nuance-approved Microphones for Mac

Here are two other retail marketplaces I found useful:

· Knowbrainer

· SpeechRecognitionSolutions

10 Considerations When Purchasing a Microphone for Dictation

To choose the best microphone for me, I found the following distinctions helpful.

1. **Dynamic Mics** tend to be more expensive than **Condenser Mics.**

2. **Condenser Mics** can pick up ambient noise and echo, to include your humming refrigerator, air in your vents, computer fans, and such, not to mention any serious environmental interference.

3. **Condenser Mics** are also more fragile, meaning not as portable.

4. **Condenser Mics** need external power or batteries (dynamic mics don't).

5. **Dynamic Mics** sacrifice quality but pick up less ambient noise. When using a **Dynamic Mic**, get right up close to it.

6. **Know Your Mic Connections**. Mic connections may be standard XLR connections (round with several pins, plugging into audio, video, or lighting equipment), or USB connections (flat or rectangular, plugging right into your computer). USB models tend to be cheaper and simpler to set up.

7. **Consider Thinking Like a Podcaster**. The reason being simply: you might end up being one sooner than you think. Why not think ahead and buy something that could work for both podcasting and speech dictation? You may also want a boom or mic stand, lead, and shock

mount (for a condenser mic). If you expect to ever have more than one person on your podcast, for example, you should consider purchasing standard XLR mics and a mixer with the ability to connect to USB (again, for connecting to your computer).

8. **Know the Tradeoffs Between Wired and Wireless.** Wired microphones tend to be more accurate while wireless give you more freedom to move around.

9. **Circumaural versus Supra-aural**. For headphones, circumaural means around the ears and supra-aural means resting on the ears. This is a matter of preference and you may want to try both kinds to see which you like.

10. **Don't Forget the DIY or Accessories.** You may be able to turn headphones you already own into a headset. Also, your mobile device may have come with earbuds with an integrated mic but these may not work because they have both incoming and outgoing audio. The result may be very quiet dictation recordings. Always test a microphone before dictating a long passage.

Comparison Chart of Affordable Wired Microphones

Also referred to as table mics, these desktop microphones are a great place to start if you don't mind more restricted mobility.

In return, you may gain more accuracy with these types of microphones.

MANUFACTURER	MODEL	ESTIMATED PRICE in USD	TYPE
Blue	Snowflake; Snowball; Yeti	50-100	Desktop
Samson	Meteor	65	Desktop
Andrea Electronics	NC-181; NC-185; NC-250v; ANC-700; ANC-750;	35-80	Headset
Jabra	BIZ 2300; BIZ 240 Duo UC; UC Voice 750; Jabra 550	70-130	Headset

Nuance	USB Dragon Headset	35	Headset
Plantronics	Audio 628; Audio 400 DSP	25-50	Headset
Sennheiser	PC330/SC 230/SC 260	80-120	Headset
SpeechWare	FlexyMike	70+	Headset
VXI Corporation	UC ProSet LUX 10/31; TalkPro UC1/UC2/UC3; TalkPro USB1/USB2/USB3	70-120	Headset

While I have summarized some cheap options, I would suggest you invest as much as you can. Here are a few more expensive options I'd look at first:

· The Audio Technica AT2020 is popular but pricier at about $230 USD. Writers will likely favor the USB model that connects right to your computer as opposed to the XLR that connects to specialty audio equipment. Tripod included.

· SpeechWare USB TableMikes are another pricier standout ($200+ USD) in wired tabletop microphones, winning such recognition from Nuance, MacWorld, MacWelt, and others. It features Speech Equaliser (EQ) and 'Automatic Gain Control (AGC)' technologies which compensate for variable distances between you and the microphone, for example. You'll see these listed on tons of 'best of' lists. SpeechWare TableMikes are helpful because they may offer you the ability to roam the room as you dictate to your desktop, though environmental factors such as background noise and your voice tonality may influence how well this will work for you. Other product lines include SpeechWare USB TravelMikes and the FlexyMike already mentioned in my chart.

· The Rode Procaster ($230+ USD) is a dynamic USB mic that features a filter to tone down plosives (or stop consonants).

In summary, more expensive microphone headsets tend to have more complete noise cancellation and can better facilitate a podcast, for example, as well as other improvements to comfort and sound quality you might prefer, but lower-end models can get speech recognition jobs done. I do not always use an external mic for dictation, but in many environments it makes sense. Invest what you can.

Comparison Chart of Affordable Wireless Microphones

With wireless speech recognition, a USB soundcard might improve your experience.

Not every wireless mic comes with one. If you're having trouble, adding a USB 'dongle' may help by providing wideband audio.

Note that Dragon also features a Bluetooth mode in some cases.

MANUFACTURER	MODEL	ESTIMATED PRICE	TYPE
Logitech	H600/H800	$50 - 60 USD	Wireless
Jabra	Pro 930	$160 USD	Wireless
Plantronics	Audio 995/ Voyager Legend UC Bluetooth	$100-200 USD	Wireless
Jabra	Pro 9465 / 9470	$200 USD	Wireless
ModMic	4.0	$50 USD	Wearable

Samson	Go Mic	$40 USD	Wireless
Zalman Clip	Zm-Mic1	$10 USD	Wearable

Again, you may find more quality and comfort and higher price points but these can typically work for speech recognition for those with tight budgets. That said, wireless mics are generally fussier than wired mics when it comes to speech recognition.

Personally, I do not use a wireless mic. I do sometimes use Dragon's remote mic app for iOS, which turns my cell phone into a mic as I roam my house.

Introduction to Working with a Human Transcriptionist

If you decide you don't want to deal with learning transcription software commands, here are some great places to start your search for human helpers, also known as transcriptionists or stenographers.

You could hire a live human transcriptionist in the very traditional sense—one who is right there in the room typing while you talk. It might be worth it to feel like Emma Thompson in the movie *Stranger Than Fiction*, dictating to Queen Latifah.

I'm going to assume the Queen is both not available and outside your budget, as are most live or real-time transcriptionists.

Most affordable transcriptionists work remotely, with you sending them digital files or cassettes and them sending you back a word processor document with your text.

15 Affordable Remote Transcription Services

Finding the right transcriptionist can be a very personal thing because your project is so important to you. Here are 14 places to start that search.

- AudioTranscription.org
- Synergy Transcription Services
- GMR Transcription
- PremiumTranscripts.com
- Casting Words
- TranscribeMe!
- TranscriptionPuppy.com
- VerbalInk.com
- Scribie.com
- TSI Transcripts
- Tigerfish
- Canadian Virtual Assistant League
- Elance
- Guru
- VWorker

You might also consider asking other dictationists for a referral or look online at writer's magazines or organizations.

Security Concerns When Working with Transcriptionists

Be sure to look for professionals who are licensed, insured, and/or bonded, and whom you can trust to not compromise your intellectual property.

Here are some associations to help out with this:

· Geographical organizations such as The American Transcription Association or The American Association of Electronic Reporters and Transcriptionists

· State or province professional licensing departments

· Local educational institutions or transcription schools who might have reputable referrals or career placement for their students

How Much You Should Expect to Pay a Transcriptionist

This absolutely varies but you can expect a professional transcriptionist to charge about $1-2 USD a minute or a rate based on each word processed page. It becomes a bit complicated because every transcription company has its own business model, but this should give you a general baseline of what to expect.

Overview of 26 Drills and 3 Skill Levels of Dictation

A couple dozen days may be long enough to get you up and running—it was in my experience, once I figured out how to approach practicing. But there's no point pressuring yourself to a time limit because each person is different. Even if it takes you the better part of year to learn to dictate, that's time well-spent and future productivity gained, but you're probably going to be surprised by how much better you get practicing just two hours a day for 24 days. Just go for it!

The Intended Format

You'll notice from the following calendar that some drills are associated with a practice excerpt. My intention is to have you do the following each day:

1. Go through the daily drill and/or excerpt (40-60 minutes)

3. Dictate your own work in progress (60-80 minutes)

The Main Objective

Remember your first typing class, doing series of 'asdf asdf asdf', etc.? Drills are an awesome way to rewire your brain, just like speed drills were when you were learning to type. Then the practice excerpts help you apply the drill further.

The goal is to become so comfortable with dictating that you do not think about it much. Instead, you think about what you are creating.

The Calendar and Order are Just Suggestions

Drills are also an awesome path for discovery. Because dictation is so foreign to most of us, some trial and error should be expected. Not everyone responds to every type of drill.

Drills are like magnifying glasses that help you create sharper learning opportunities for yourself. Customize your practice to what's working for you while not being too easy on yourself. Please choose exercises that stretch you rather than becoming another dictation casualty.

The two most powerful warriors are patience and time. - Leo Tolstoy

Also, this is not elegant or relaxing practice. This is the kind of practice where you're doing something you're functionally klunky at, as opposed to something you're already fairly amazing at and striving for polish or perfection.

If there's anything I know from more than a decade teaching business and office productivity classes, it's that learning doesn't happen when you're in your comfort zone. It happens when you are stretched past it.

Not for You? Here's Why You Should At Least Skim These Drills

Even if you don't do these exercises, at least do yourself the favor of scanning through them because they serve as a list of ways to dictate with more speed and finesse. Any one of them could be the kingpin that really knocks down dictation barriers for your brain.

Why These Drills Were Written for Dragon Commands

As I put this together, I found it inconceivable to delineate commands for every program out there. Most writers are going to choose Dragon, so my examples for the first several drills and practice excerpts are in terms of the commands for the desktop Windows version of Dragon NaturallySpeaking 13, as they function on my laptop. If you end up using something else, you may have to adapt individual commands a bit.

Finally, if a given command isn't working, programs like Dragon often have alternates. Search for these under the program's Help option or in the program's online documentation.

My Drills Are Not the Boss of You

Some of these may seem kooky to you, and that's fine. I am a kooky person and these represent what worked for me. Don't knock them until you try them!

I taught keyboarding for several years at the college level. I always felt this was different than teaching younger typists. Many of my students have felt a lot of resistance mentally to learning something new.

Maybe that's what I drew on when I faced resistance at learning this new skill of dictation. I was *so slow*. It occurred to me, why not approach this the same way we learned to type? When you do keyboarding drills, you practice letter combinations. You practice sentence elements like words or phrases with basic punctuation. Then you practice whole sentences, and finally add in numbers, special punctuation, and special symbols. Some methodologies also added in mid-sentence editing and such for word processing as opposed to merely typing.

That's what I've created here, in this 3-phase system of drills:

· Level 1: Basic Commands (Drills 1-8) – Capitalization, Punctuation, Numbers, Navigation, Corrections, and more

· Level 2: Verbal Storytelling (Drills 9-16) – Practice retelling or describing verbally rather than by typing or handwriting

· Level 3: Creative Flow (Drills 17-26) – Creative writing drills relating to your work in progress

You can just sit and dictate your work in progress if you would rather, but I suggest going through drills 1-8 at a minimum.

It's all about discovery, narrowing down what works for you. No one can tell you that, but I can offer you a quick and methodical way to explore.

4 Week Calendar for Dictation Drills

"Know thyself."

— Socrates

In this sample calendar, I give one day off each week from doing drills and kept it simple, but it's all just a suggestion. Again, each of us assimilates this kind of technical skill at a different rate. This is a map for how to practice for two hours a day, reach any NaNoWriMo goals you might have (50,000 words in a month), and learn to dictate.

In the chart, "WIP" refers to your work in progress, such as a story or novel.

Shown on next page. Some devices may require that you rotate your screen long-ways to see all columns.

DAY 1	DAY 2	DAY 3	DAY 4	DAY 5	DAY 6	WIP Totals
Prep Drill Drill 1 Practice Excerpt 1 WIP (1,000 words)	Drill 2 Practice Excerpt 2 WIP (2,000 words)	Drill 3 Practice Excerpt 3 WIP (2,000 words)	Drill 4 Practice Excerpt 4 WIP (2,000 words)	Drill 5 Practice Excerpt 5 WIP (2,000 words)	Drill 6 Practice Excerpt 6 WIP (2,000 words)	11,000 WORDS

DAY 7	DAY 8	DAY 9	DAY 10	DAY 11	DAY 12	
Drill 7 Practice Excerpt 7 WIP (2,000 words)	Drill 8 Practice Excerpt 8 WIP (2,000 words)	Drill 9 WIP (2,500 words)	Drill 10 WIP (2,500 words)	Drill 11 WIP (2,500 words)	Drill 12 WIP (2,500 words)	25,000 WORDS

DAY 13	DAY 14	DAY 15	DAY 16	DAY 17	DAY 18	
Drill 13 WIP (2,500 words)	Drill 14 WIP (2,500 words)	Drill 15 WIP (2,500 words)	Drill 16 WIP (2,500 words)	Drill 17 WIP (2,500 words)	Drill 18 WIP (2,500 words)	40,000 WORDS
DAY 19	DAY 20	DAY 21	DAY 22	DAY 23	DAY 24	
Drill 19 WIP (2,500 words)	Drill 20 WIP (2,500 words)	Drill 21 WIP (2,500 words)	Drill 22 WIP (2,500 words)	Drill 23 Drill 24 WIP (2,500 words)	Drill 25 Drill 26 WIP (2,500 words)	55,000 WORDS

Pep Talk: 5 Things to Tell Yourself When You Get Discouraged

"All Moanday, Tearday, Wailsday, Thumpsday, Frightday, Shatterday." — James Joyce

James Joyce pretty much summed up the initial dictation experience. Plan on it feeling like you're slogging through mud. You will of course get better! Until then, you might need a few points of perspective:

1. You're a writer. You're probably overly hard on yourself.

"A man of genius makes no mistakes. His errors are volitional and are the portals of discovery." — James Joyce, Ulysses

2. **It's not personal. It's simply the stuff of rewiring.** Learning to dictate, like many things, might lead you to feel personally inept. It's not about your personal worth as a writer or human being. Changing something as fundamental as how you communicate simply takes some due diligence. You're retraining the connections between mental and lingual capacities, not to mention how all that links to your creative process.

3. **You did not become a handwriter or typist in one session.** It took you the larger part of kindergarten or first grade for the former and a dedicated keyboarding class or study program for the latter. If you could learn those things then you can certainly learn to dictate now.

In fact, comparatively, dictating comes pretty naturally because it is natural. We all tell stories, or used to as kids. For me, dictation took several weeks of practicing for at least two hours per day, with more polish coming in subsequent months, but I was functionally dictating after mere weeks, which is pretty amazing. So don't get too impatient.

4. **The QWERTY was designed to slow you down**. Saying what you think is simpler than thinking something, then moving your hands accordingly across a QWERTY keyboard configuration—which I've already mentioned was arranged with the aim of slowing typists down so that typewriter keys wouldn't jam so often, and yet we still stay entrenched in our old ways instead of adopting something like the DVORAK configuration! Comparatively, just speaking something, even if you have to learn tags for punctuation and such, has a certain elegance to it. Talking is actually a much more natural skill—or at least was acquired earlier for most of us. My theory is that typing and handwriting only feel more natural because of repetition rather than innate ease.

5. **Your initial reactions might not be serving you well on this one.** Most people would acknowledge that the body and mind resist a lot of natural, good things. Inner resistance isn't always an indication that you should give up.

Preparation: Opening the Program, Starting or Stopping Dictation, and Opening or Closing Files

To begin, begin.

— William Wordsworth

Objective: To practice starting and stopping the dictation software with your voice, as well as searching and opening files.

This drill runs you through the fundamentals of getting started with dictation and assumes you have already download dictation software then gone through any voice acclimation wizards or tutorials you were prompted to do upon installation.

* If you don't have a desktop version of Dragon yet, try <u>a free online dictation program</u> to help you decide if you like dictation. Or, download a mobile app, as discussed earlier in this book.

As a reminder, for sanity's sake, I had to choose one dictation program as a baseline and Dragon was the obvious choice. Commands in other programs may differ.

1. Open a program like Microsoft Word. This is what you will type in.

2. Open the dictation program. Some dictation programs can be launched with your voice. [Start Microsoft Word / WordPerfect, etc]. I have more success opening Dragon manually. The Dragon Bar should then pop up with a Go button right in the center. Select this to start dictating.

3. After that, you can do a whole bunch of navigational or functional voice commands for things you used to do with keyboard shortcuts or mouse clicking.

Say the following and watch what happens in your document:

Open New File

Close File

Note that you cannot dictate the Save / Not Save dialog box in Microsoft Word, which is a safety measure. Click 'Don't Save'.

Open File

In Word 2013, I could not dictate file names, but give this a try to see if you can:

My Documents

[Say the name of an existing file]

Close File

Open New File

Save File

Same thing here. In Word 2013, the Dragon Bar gives me the message that I cannot dictate the particulars of the save. I have to click where and what to name the file. You can, however say [Save Changes] once you have established a file location and name.

this is my first dictation and i am already loving it

Save Changes

Set Page Orientation to Landscape View

Set Page Orientation to Portrait View

Hide Ruler

Show Ruler

Zoom to fifty percent

Zoom to one hundred percent (*if you say 'a hundred percent' it won't work*)

Preview the File

Close the Preview Show Paragraph Marks

Hide Paragraph Marks

Print Document (*you may have to manually close this dialog box if you don't actually want to print*)

Check Spelling or Check Grammar (*then you would say Skip Once, Skip All, Replace or Add*)

(*Close dialog boxes*)

Select [say a word in your document]

Check Thesaurus

(Close dialog boxes)

New Line

Insert Page Break

Page Up

Line Down

Line Up

Page Down

Go to Top

Go to Bottom

Go Back *(this was a fussy command for me; you have say this fairly quickly after the last command, to return to the previous place)*

Now you're ready for a few tips!

Time to Dictate: 15 General Guidelines for Working with Speech to Text Software

We have gone over several of these points earlier in the book, but here's a quick reminder of some best practices for dictating.

1. **Don't share, or be careful how you do.** Because you train the software, don't share the software with others without creating a new user profile (a feature not available in all dictation programs).

2. **Quiet environments work best, but every device performs differently** – It sounds like common sense but may not be when you're learning something new. Watch out for rustling papers, background music, phone calls, or other immediate or background noise. Be aware of nervous ticks like breathing in sharply or thumping your fingers on the desk and such. I confused my first several recordings royally by sniffing and lost data. All this said, you may be able to do more than you think in noisy environments, so play with that as well.

3. **Keep checking**. Know whether your recording device is on and in record mode. It really stinks to put in an hour of work just to realize your recorder was never turned on or its batteries are dead.

4. **Enunciate.** Depending on your program or device you may need to learn to emphasize consonants in an exaggerated way.

7. **Don't annunciate.** As in, speaking very loudly. Why? It usually creates fuzz factor.

5. **Speak evenly.** Avoid crazy inflection where your tones change a lot, although I have been surprised how much I can get away with.

6. **Moderate your speed.** You don't need to speak especially slowly, but speaking too quickly may lead to errors.

8. **Consider titling or introducing dictations**. This is a good habit to get into because it allows some programs to search for that dictation later on.

9. **Consider announcing the end of a dictation.** Similarly, it's a good habit to say 'end of dictation' for courtesy to a transcriptionist or searchability in a digital file.

10. **Minimize pauses**. Some pausing is fine but long pauses may cause the software to time out. You can always stop and start the recording to ameliorate this.

11. **Use voice tags for research.** Have a system for things you want to come back to later. Again, don't stop and look things up. Dictation is all about flow.

12. **Experiment with distance.** Change up the distance from your mouth to the microphone or digital recorder to see what gives you the most accuracy.

13. **Experiment with sentence length.** Some programs favor shorter sentences over longer. Knowing this can help you alleviate time-outs. I haven't needed to worry about this but it's worth mentioning.

14. **Don't worry about grammar, passive voice or other stylistic concerns.** Just tell the story. You'll likely be surprised by how readable your dictation turns out to be.

15. Throw out punctuation or capitalization commands that drive you batty! I advocate getting better at each command, but if you can't stand saying [Open Quote] [Close Quote] each time your characters talk, throw it out and put those in later, rather than just giving up on dictation.

Dictation Drill 1: Punctuation & Capitalization Commands

"She feels in italics and thinks in CAPITALS." — Henry James

Objective: To become more adept at dictating punctuation marks within a document.

Unless you are trying to rival James Joyce's *Ulysses*, the final episode "Penelope" coming in at over 24,000 words and only 3 punctuation marks, your dictation will be so much easier to edit later if it includes commas, periods, and capitalization.

· Go through the following commands, which have been repeated in different sequences, repeating the entire drill once or several times as you see fit while paying attention to what happens to the text on your screen.

· Again, this may feel tedious, but it really only takes a couple minutes and by speaking the commands and seeing what happens, you will create a mental anchor. The idea is for these commands to then come to mind more readily when you are authoring a document of your own.

· Note that many capitalization commands will not work in Dragon if you have your Caps Lock on.

· You may need to check the Vocabulary Editor to change a few settings. You can add often capitalized phrases (such as The Pennington Group) or to always capitalize the first word in a new line, for example. The following drills assume that your settings are default.

Say the following and watch what happens:

Period

Comma

Colon

Semi-colon

Ellipsis

Apostrophe

Exclamation Mark

Question Mark

Ampersand

Hyphen

Dash

Open Quote

Close Quote

Open Parenthesis

Close Parenthesis

Cap

[Say your favorite food] is amazing

Caps On

[Say another favorite food] is amazing

Caps Off

[Say another favorite food] is amazing

All Caps On

[Say another favorite food] is amazing

All caps off

[Say another favorite food] is amazing

Cap That

Next run through the following practice excerpt, speaking all commands. This will be followed by an unprompted version of the same passage, to see if you can dictate it without help. As you do this, try to see a punctuation mark and the tag as one unit, impressing the relationship on your brain.

Practice Excerpt 1 with Prompts: From Alice's Adventures in Wonderland, Lewis Carroll

When I created these dictation tags, I only listed those the software demanded of me. For example, Queen and Alice were automatically capitalized so just know you may or may not have to say 'Cap' before some names and, apart from quotations, you shouldn't have to [Cap] the first word of a sentence. You do not have to speak spaces. You do not have to speak apostrophes in conjunctions. If any words are misspelled just move on; we learn spelling and correction in a later drill. Finally, because these excerpts come from classics, some of the language and usage can be a bit different from what we use today, so don't stress about that.

[Cap]The chief difficulty [Cap]Alice found at first was in managing her flamingo:[Colon] she succeeded in getting its body tucked away,[Comma] comfortably enough,[Comma] under her arm,[Comma] with its legs hanging down,[Comma] but generally,[Comma] just as she had got its neck nicely straightened out,[Comma] and was going to give the hedgehog a blow with its head,[Comma] it would twist itself round and look up in her face,[Comma] with such a puzzled expression that she could not help bursting out laughing:[Colon] and when she had got its head down,[Comma] and was going to begin again,[Comma] it was very provoking to find that the hedgehog had unrolled itself,[Comma] and was in the act of crawling away:[Colon] besides all this,[Comma] there was generally a ridge or furrow in the way wherever she wanted to send the hedgehog to,[Comma] and,[Comma] as the doubled- [Hyphen] up soldiers were always getting up and walking off to other parts of the ground,[Comma] [Cap]Alice soon came to the conclusion that it was a very difficult game indeed.[Period] [New Line]

[Cap]The players all played at once without waiting for turns,[Comma] quarrelling all the while,[Comma] and fighting for the hedgehogs;[Semicolon] and in a very short time the Queen was in a furious passion,[Comma] and went stamping about,[Comma] and shouting "[Open Quote][Cap]Off with his head![Exclamation Mark] " [Close Quote] or "[Open Quote] [Cap]Off with her head![Exclamation Mark] " [Close Quote] about once in a minute.[Period] [New Line]

[Cap]Alice began to feel very uneasy:[Colon] to be sure,[Comma] she had not as yet had any dispute with the [Cap]Queen,[Comma] but she knew that it might happen any minute,[Comma] "[Open Quote]and then,[Comma] " [Close Quote] thought she,[Comma] "[Open Quote] what would become of me? [Question Mark] [Cap]They're dreadfully fond of beheading people here;[Semicolon] the great wonder is,[Comma] that there's any one left alive! [Exclamation Mark] " [Close Quote] [New Line]

[Cap]She was looking about for some way of escape,[Comma] and wondering whether she could get away without being seen,[Comma] when she noticed a curious appearance in the air:[Colon] it puzzled her very much at first,[Comma] but,[Comma] after watching it a minute or two,[Comma] she made it out to be a grin,[Comma] and she said to herself "[Open Quote] [Cap]It's the [Cap]Cheshire [Cap]Cat:[Colon] now I shall have somebody to talk to.[Period] "[Close Quote] [New Line]

"[Open Quote][Cap]How are you getting on ?[Question Mark] "[Close Quote] said the [Cap]Cat,[Comma] as soon as there was mouth enough for it to speak with.[Period] [New Line]

[Cap]Alice waited till the eyes appeared,[Comma] and then nodded.[Period] "[Open Quote] [Cap]It's no use speaking to it,[Comma] " [Close Quote] she thought,[Comma] "[Open Quote]till its ears have come,[Comma] or at least one of them.[Period] " [Close Quote] In another minute the whole head appeared,[Comma] and then [Cap]Alice put down her flamingo,[Comma] and began an account of the game,[Comma] feeling very glad she had someone to listen to her.[Period] The [Cap]Cat seemed to think that there was enough of it now in sight,[Comma] and no more of it appeared.[Period] [New Line]

"[Open Quote] I don't think they play at all fairly,[Comma] " [Close Quote] [Cap]Alice began,[Comma] in rather a complaining tone,[Comma] "[Open Quote] and they all quarrel so dreadfully one can't hear oneself speak— [Dash] and they don't seem to have any rules in particular;[Semicolon] at least,[Comma] if there are,[Comma] nobody attends to them— [Dash] and you've no idea how confusing it is all the things being alive;[Semicolon] for instance,[Comma] there's the arch I've got to go through next walking about at the other end of the ground— [Dash] and I should have croqueted the [Cap]Queen's hedgehog just now,[Comma] only it ran away when it saw mine coming! [Exclamation Mark] "[Close Quote] [New Line]

"[Open Quote][Cap]How do you like the Queen? [Question Mark] "[Close Quote] said[Lowercase That] the [Cap]Cat in a low voice.[Period] [New Line]

"[Open Quote] [Cap]Not at all,[Comma] "[Close Quote] said [Cap]Alice:[Colon] "[Open Quote] she's so extremely— [Dash] "[Close Quote] [Cap]Just then she noticed that the Queen was close behind her,[Comma] listening:[Colon] so she went on,[Comma] "[Open Quote]— [Dash] likely to win,[Comma] that it's hardly worth while finishing the game.[Period] "[Close Quote] [New Line]

The [Cap]Queen smiled and passed on. [Period]

Now try the same excerpt without prompts...

Practice Excerpt 1 without Prompts: From Alice's Adventures in Wonderland, Lewis Carroll

The chief difficulty Alice found at first was in managing her flamingo: she succeeded in getting its body tucked away, comfortably enough, under her arm, with its legs hanging down, but generally, just as she had got its neck nicely straightened out, and was going to give the hedgehog a blow with its head, it would twist itself round and look up in her face, with such a puzzled expression that she could not help bursting out laughing: and when she had got its head down, and was going to begin again, it was very provoking to find that the hedgehog had unrolled itself, and was in the act of crawling away: besides all this, there was generally a ridge or furrow in the way wherever she wanted to send the hedgehog to, and, as the doubled-up soldiers were always getting up and walking off to other parts of the ground, Alice soon came to the conclusion that it was a very difficult game indeed.

The players all played at once without waiting for turns, quarrelling all the while, and fighting for the hedgehogs; and in a very short time the Queen was in a furious passion, and went stamping about, and shouting "Off with his head!" or "Off with her head!" about once in a minute.

Alice began to feel very uneasy: to be sure, she had not as yet had any dispute with the Queen, but she knew that it might happen any minute, "and then," thought she, "what would become of me? They're dreadfully fond of beheading people here; the great wonder is, that there's any one left alive!"

She was looking about for some way of escape, and wondering whether she could get away without being seen, when she noticed a curious appearance in the air: it puzzled her very much at first, but, after watching it a minute or two, she made it out to be a grin, and she said to herself "It's the Cheshire Cat: now I shall have somebody to talk to."

"How are you getting on?" said the Cat, as soon as there was mouth enough for it to speak with.

Alice waited till the eyes appeared, and then nodded. "It's no use speaking to it," she thought, "till its ears have come, or at least one of them." In another minute the whole head appeared, and then Alice put down her flamingo, and began an account of the game, feeling very glad she had someone to listen to her. The Cat seemed to think that there was enough of it now in sight, and no more of it appeared.

"I don't think they play at all fairly," Alice began, in rather a complaining tone, "and they all quarrel so dreadfully one can't hear oneself speak—and they don't seem to have any rules in particular; at least, if there are, nobody attends to them—and you've no idea how confusing it is all the things being alive; for instance, there's the arch I've got to go through next walking about at the other end of the ground—and I should have croqueted the Queen's hedgehog just now, only it ran away when it saw mine coming!"

"How do you like the Queen?" said the Cat in a low voice.

"Not at all," said Alice: "she's so extremely—"Just then she noticed that the Queen was close behind her, listening: so she went on, "—likely to win, that it's hardly worth while finishing the game."

The Queen smiled and passed on.

That's it for this drill and excerpt! If it felt goopy, that's par for the course.

*Now, just open your work in progress and dictate **2,000** words! I know how that sounds, but it will go faster than you think. Even if you have to speak very slowly and don't particularly like what you're coming up with, get to that **2,000** word goal. I suggest timing yourself without feeling pressured, just so you know how long it takes you to get to **2,000** words.*

My advice is to not stop to correct errors as you dictate, go back and do it after.

If you'd like, read through it and correct it afterward. Or don't even look at it until the end of the month. Up to you!

Dictation Drill 2: Spelling Out Proper Nouns or Unusual Words

"Our torments also may in length of time

Become our Elements." — John Milton, Paradise Lost

Objective: To become proficient at spelling out names, places, and other unique words the dictation software is not likely to recognize.

Keep in mind you can add often-used names, such as your characters' names, by adding them as entries in the vocabulary tool.

In Dragon, the Spelling Window is where you add new words for more accuracy when you try to dictate it again. Here's how that's done:

1. Say a word, then immediately after, say [Spell That].

2. You can then either spell the word the way you would like it, choose one of the program's guesses by saying the coordinating number, play it back to yourself, or train the program further. For this drill, we're just spelling things out.

Say your first name

Even if it spells it right say [Spell That] (a window should pop up)

Beginning with [Cap] then the first letter, spell your first name in letters

[Okay]

Say your last name

[Spell That]

Beginning with [Cap] then the first letter, spell your last name in letters

[Okay]

Think of the name of a school you went to, assuming it has more than one word in the name

Say the first word in the school's name

Beginning with [Cap] then the first letter, spell the first word in the school's name

[Okay or Choose [1,2,3, etc]]

Say the second word in the school's name

Beginning with [Cap] then the first letter, spell your last name in letters

[Okay or Choose [1,2,3, etc]]

Repeat for any other words in the school's name

[Select Word] (a word should be highlighted)

[Spell That]

Beginning with [Cap] then the first letter, spell it
again in letters.

[Okay or Choose [1,2,3, etc]]

[Select [your first name]] (it should be
highlighted)

[Spell That]

Beginning with [Cap] then the first letter, spell
your first name in letters

[Okay or Choose [1,2,3, etc]]

You can continue this by making a list of everyone in
your family, places you'd like to travel, or any other
group of capitalized words, or move on to the practice
excerpt.

You'll also learn about Spell Mode in the next drill.

Practice Excerpt 2 with Prompts: from The Jungle Book by Rudyard Kipling

In the following excerpt I've used the [Spell That] tag. When you see it, say [Spell That] then [Cap] and spell the name, then say Choose [1,2,3,etc].

"[Open Quote][Cap]And what is a man that he should not run with his brothers?[Question Mark] "[Close Quote] said Mowgli [Spell That].[Period] "[Open Quote] I was born in the jungle.[Period] I have obeyed the [Cap]Law of the [Cap]Jungle, [Comma] and there is no wolf of ours from whose paws I have not pulled a thorn.[Period] Surely they are my brothers![Exclamation Mark] "[Close Quote] [New Line]

Bagheera[Spell That] stretched himself at full length and half shut his eyes.[Period] "[Open Quote][Cap]Little [Cap]Brother,[Comma] "[Close Quote] said he,[Comma] "[Open Quote]feel under my jaw[Spell That].[Period] "[Close Quote] [New Line]

Mowgli put up his strong brown hand,[Comma] and just under Bagheera's silky chin,[Comma] where the giant rolling muscles were all hid by the glossy hair,[Comma] he came upon a little bald spot.[Period] [New Line]

"[Open Quote][Cap]There is no one in the jungle that knows that I,[Comma] Bagheera,[Comma] carry that mark—[Dash]the mark of the collar[Spell That];[Semicolon] and yet,[Comma] [Cap]Little [Cap]Brother,[Comma] I was born among men,[Comma] and it was among men that my mother died—[Dash]in the cages of the king's palace at Oodeypore.[Period] It was because of this that I paid the price for thee at the [Cap]Council when thou wast a little naked cub.[Period] Yes,[Comma] I too was born among men.[Period] I had never seen the jungle.[Period] They fed me behind bars from an iron pan till one night I felt that I was Bagheera—[Dash] the [Cap]Panther—[Dash]and no man's plaything,[Comma] and I broke the silly lock with one blow of my paw and came away.[Period] And because I had learned the ways of men,[Comma] I became more terrible in the jungle than Shere Khan[Spell That].[Period] Is it not so?[Question Mark] "[Close Quote] [New Line]

"[Open Quote]Yes, [Comma]"[Close Quote] said Mowgli,[Comma] "[Open Quote]all the jungle fear Bagheera—[Dash]all except Mowgli. [Period]"[Close Quote] [New Line]

"[Open Quote]Oh,[Comma] thou art a man's cub, [Comma]"[Close Quote] said the [Cap]Black [Cap]Panther very tenderly.[Period] "[Open Quote]And even as I returned to my jungle,[Comma] so thou must go back to men at last—[Dash]to the men who are thy brothers—[Dash]if thou art not killed in the [Cap]Council. [Period]"[Close Quote] [New Line]

"[Open Quote]But why—[Dash]but why should any wish to kill me?[Question Mark] "[Close Quote] said Mowgli.[Period] [New Line]

"[Open Quote]Look at me, [Comma]"[Close Quote] said Bagheera.[Period] And Mowgli looked at him steadily between the eyes.[Period] The big panther turned his head away in half a minute.[Period] [New Line]

"[Open Quote]That is why, [Comma]"[Close Quote] he said,[Comma] shifting his paw on the leaves.[Period] "[Open Quote]Not even I can look thee between the eyes,[Comma] and I was born among men,[Comma] and I love thee,[Comma] [Cap]Little [Cap]Brother.[Period] The others they hate thee because their eyes cannot meet thine;[Semicolon] because thou art wise;[Semicolon] because thou hast pulled out thorns from their feet—[Dash]because thou art a man. [Period]"[Close Quote] [New Line]

"[Open Quote]I did not know these things, [Comma]"[Close Quote] said Mowgli sullenly,[Comma] and he frowned under his heavy black eyebrows.[Period] [New Line]

"[Open Quote]What is the [Cap]Law of the [Cap]Jungle ? [Question Mark] Strike first and then give tongue.[Period] By thy very carelessness they know that thou art a man.[Period] But be wise.[Period] It is in my heart that when Akela[Spell That] misses his next kill— [Dash]and at each hunt it costs him more to pin the buck—[Dash]the [Cap]Pack will turn against him and against thee.[Period] They will hold a jungle Council at the Rock,[Comma] and then—[Dash]and then—[Dash]I have it![Exclamation Mark]"[Close Quote] said Bagheera,[Comma] leaping up.[Period] "[Open Quote]Go thou down quickly to the men's huts in the valley,[Comma] and take some of the [Cap]Red [Cap]Flower which they grow there,[Comma] so that when the time comes thou mayest have even a stronger friend than I or Baloo[Spell That] or those of the [Cap]Pack that love thee.[Period] Get the [Cap]Red [Cap]Flower. [Period]"[Close Quote] [New Line]

By [Cap]Red [Cap]Flower Bagheera meant fire,[Comma] only no creature in the jungle will call fire by its proper name.[Period] Every beast lives in deadly fear of it,[Comma] and invents a hundred ways of describing it.[Period] [New Line]

"[Open Quote]The [Cap]Red [Cap]Flower? [Question Mark] "[Close Quote] said Mowgli.[Period] "[Open Quote]That grows outside their huts in the twilight.[Period] I will get some. [Period]"[Close Quote] [New Line]

"[Open Quote]There speaks the man's cub, [Comma]"[Close Quote] said Bagheera proudly.[Period] "[Open Quote]Remember that it grows in little pots.[Period] Get one swiftly,[Comma] and keep it by thee for time of need. [Period]"[Close Quote] [New Line]

Practice Excerpt 2 without Prompts: from The Jungle Book by Rudyard Kipling

"And what is a man that he should not run with his brothers?" said Mowgli. "I was born in the jungle. I have obeyed the Law of the Jungle, and there is no wolf of ours from whose paws I have not pulled a thorn. Surely they are my brothers!"

Bagheera stretched himself at full length and half shut his eyes. "Little Brother," said he, "feel under my jaw."

Mowgli put up his strong brown hand, and just under Bagheera's silky chin, where the giant rolling muscles were all hid by the glossy hair, he came upon a little bald spot.

"There is no one in the jungle that knows that I, Bagheera, carry that mark—the mark of the collar; and yet, Little Brother, I was born among men, and it was among men that my mother died—in the cages of the king's palace at Oodeypore. It was because of this that I paid the price for thee at the Council when thou wast a little naked cub. Yes, I too was born among men. I had never seen the jungle. They fed me behind bars from an iron pan till one night I felt that I was Bagheera—the Panther—and no man's plaything, and I broke the silly lock with one blow of my paw and came away. And because I had learned the ways of men, I became more terrible in the jungle than Shere Khan. Is it not so?"

"Yes," said Mowgli, "all the jungle fear Bagheera—all except Mowgli."

"Oh, thou art a man's cub," said the Black Panther very tenderly. "And even as I returned to my jungle, so thou must go back to men at last—to the men who are thy brothers—if thou art not killed in the Council."

"But why—but why should any wish to kill me?" said Mowgli.

"Look at me," said Bagheera. And Mowgli looked at him steadily between the eyes. The big panther turned his head away in half a minute.

"That is why," he said, shifting his paw on the leaves. "Not even I can look thee between the eyes, and I was born among men, and I love thee, Little Brother. The others they hate thee because their eyes cannot meet thine; because thou art wise; because thou hast pulled out thorns from their feet—because thou art a man."

"I did not know these things," said Mowgli sullenly, and he frowned under his heavy black eyebrows.

"What is the Law of the Jungle? Strike first and then give tongue. By thy very carelessness they know that thou art a man. But be wise. It is in my heart that when Akela misses his next kill—and at each hunt it costs him more to pin the buck—the Pack will turn against him and against thee. They will hold a jungle Council at the Rock, and then—and then—I have it!" said Bagheera, leaping up. "Go thou down quickly to the men's huts in the valley, and take some of the Red Flower which they grow there, so that when the time comes thou mayest have even a stronger friend than I or Baloo or those of the Pack that love thee. Get the Red Flower."

By Red Flower Bagheera meant fire, only no creature in the jungle will call fire by its proper name. Every beast lives in deadly fear of it, and invents a hundred ways of describing it.

"The Red Flower?" said Mowgli. "That grows outside their huts in the twilight. I will get some."

"There speaks the man's cub," said Bagheera proudly. "Remember that it grows in little pots. Get one swiftly, and keep it by thee for time of need."

You're done! Next step: Dictate 2,000 words in your work in progress.

Dictation Drill 3: Dictating Numbers and Alphanumeric Content

"Even in the valley of the shadow of death, two and two do not make six." — Leo Tolstoy

Objective: To practice how dictating numbers works in your dictation program.

In Dragon you will find a Numbers Mode and a Spell Mode (for alphanumeric). Use Numbers mode for filling in a table, for example.

1. Due to writing conventions, Dragon will interpret numbers less than 10 as a word but you can override that by saying [Numeral] before the number.

2. To change to the other modes, you can say [Spell Mode] or [Numbers Mode].

3. You can also dictate numeric descriptors like percentage or currency by using the word "sign".

Say the following:

Four

Numeral Four

Seven

Numeral Seven

Nine

[Numeral Nine] [Period]

Three

Numeral Three

Twenty [Percent Sign]

Four thousand twenty dollars and fifty five cents

Eleven point five percent

Seven hundred twenty three dollars and sixty
eight cents

chapter 1

[Cap]Chapter 1

Practice Excerpt 3 with Prompts: History of the Plague in London by Daniel Defoe

Many numbers you can just say, as you will see in this passage. To correct numbers that appear in the wrong form you can use [Spell That].

[Cap]It was about the beginning of September,[Comma] 1664,[Comma] that I,[Comma] among the rest of my neighbors,[Comma] heard in ordinary discourse that the plague was returned again in Holland;[Semicolon] for it had been very violent there...[Elipsis] [New Line]

[Cap]We had no such thing as printed newspapers in those days,[Comma] to spread rumors and reports of things,[Comma] and to improve them by the invention of men,[Comma] as I have lived to see practiced since.[Period] But such things as those were gathered from the letters of merchants and others who corresponded abroad,[Comma] and from them was handed about by word of mouth only;[Semicolon] so that things did not spread instantly over the whole nation,[Comma] as they do now.[Period] But it seems that 18th government had a true account of it,[Comma] and several counsels were held about ways to prevent its coming over;[Semicolon] but all was kept very private.[Period] Hence it was that this rumor died off again;[Semicolon] and people began to forget it,[Comma] as a thing we were very little concerned in and that we hoped was not true,[Comma] till the latter end of November or the beginning of December,[Comma] 1664,[Comma] when two men,[Comma] said to be Frenchmen,[Comma] died of the plague in [Cap]Longacre,[Comma] or rather at the upper end of [Cap]Drury [Cap]Lane...[Elipsis][New Line]

[Cap]The usual number of burials within the bills of mortality for a week was from about two [Space] hundred [Space] and [Space] forty [Space] [or use: Spell That],[Comma] or thereabouts,[Comma] to three [Space] hundred[or use: Spell That]...[Elipsis][New Line]

[Cap]This last bill was really frightful,[Comma] being a higher number than had been known to have been buried in one week since the preceding visitation of 1656.[Period] [New Line]

[Cap]However,[Comma] all this went off again;[Semicolon] and the weather proving cold,[Comma] and the frost,[Comma] which began in December,[Comma] still continuing very severe,[Comma] even till near the end of February,[Comma] attended with sharp though moderate winds,[Comma] the bills decreased again,[Comma] and the city grew healthy;[Semicolon] and everybody began to look upon the danger as good as over,[Comma] only that still the burials in St. Giles'[Apostrophe] continued high.[Period] From the beginning of April,[Comma] especially,[Comma] they stood at twenty-five[Spell That] each week,[Comma] till the week from the 18th to the 25th,[Comma] when there was 13 buried in St.Giles'[Apostrophe] [Cap]Parish thirty[Spell That],[Comma] whereof two of the plague,[Comma] and eight of the spotted fever ([Open Parenthesis] which was looked upon as the same thing)[Close Parenthesis];[Semicolon] likewise the number that died of the spotted fever in the whole increased,[Comma] being eight the week before,[Comma] and twelve[Spell That] the week above named.[Period][New Line]

[Cap]This alarmed us all again;[Semicolon] and terrible apprehensions were among the people,[Comma] especially the weather being now changed and growing warm,[Comma] and the summer being at hand.[Period] However,[Comma] the next week there seemed to be some hopes again:[Colon] the bills were low;[Semicolon] the number of the dead in all was but 388;[Semicolon] there was none of the plague,[Comma] and but four of the spotted fever.[Period]

Practice Excerpt 3 without Prompts: History of the Plague in London by Daniel Defoe

It was about the beginning of September, 1664, that I, among the rest of my neighbors, heard in ordinary discourse that the plague was returned again in Holland; for it had been very violent there...

We had no such thing as printed newspapers in those days, to spread rumors and reports of things, and to improve them by the invention of men, as I have lived to see practiced since. But such things as those were gathered from the letters of merchants and others who corresponded abroad, and from them was handed about by word of mouth only; so that things did not spread instantly over the whole nation, as they do now. But it seems that 18th government had a true account of it, and several counsels were held about ways to prevent its coming over; but all was kept very private. Hence it was that this rumor died off again; and people began to forget it, as a thing we were very little concerned in and that we hoped was not true, till the latter end of November or the beginning of December, 1664, when two men, said to be Frenchmen, died of the plague in Longacre, or rather at the upper end of Drury Lane...

The usual number of burials within the bills of mortality for a week was from about two hundred and forty, or thereabouts, to three hundred...

This last bill was really frightful, being a higher number than had been known to have been buried in one week since the preceding visitation of 1656.

However, all this went off again; and the weather proving cold, and the frost, which began in December, still continuing very severe, even till near the end of February, attended with sharp though moderate winds, the bills decreased again, and the city grew healthy; and everybody began to look upon the danger as good as over, only that still the burials in St. Giles' continued high. From the beginning of April, especially, they stood at twenty-five each week, till the week from the 18th to the 25th, when there was 13 buried in St. Giles' Parish thirty, whereof two of the plague, and eight of the spotted fever (which was looked upon as the same thing); likewise the number that died of the spotted fever in the whole increased, being eight the week before, and twelve the week above named.

This alarmed us all again; and terrible apprehensions were among the people, especially the weather being now changed and growing warm, and the summer being at hand. However, the next week there seemed to be some hopes again: the bills were low; the number of the dead in all was but 388; there was none of the plague, and but four of the spotted fever.

*You're done! Next step: Dictate **2,000** words in your work in progress.*

Dictation Drill 4: Text Selection Commands

"I am tomorrow, or some future day, what I establish today. I am today what I established yesterday or some previous day."

— James Joyce

Objective: To become more adept at selecting text within a document.

So much of creating a document involves selecting text so you can apply other commands to that selection.

Try speaking these commands, in a document with several paragraphs of text already typed.

Select previous paragraph

Select next paragraph

Select all

Select [SAY A PHRASE FROM YOUR DOCUMENT]

Select next 3 words

Select all

Unselect that

Select line

Select next line

Select previous line

Select next 5 words

Select paragraph

Select [SAY A PHRASE FROM YOUR DOCUMENT]

Unselect that

Select previous paragraph

Select next paragraph

Select paragraph

Select all

Unselect that

Select previous 10 words

Select [SAY A PHRASE FROM YOUR DOCUMENT]

Unselect that

Select paragraph

Select word

Select previous word

Select next word

Select all

Select line

Select previous line

Select next line

Select paragraph

Select next paragraph

Select previous paragraph

Practice Excerpt 4 with Prompts: from Jane Eyre by Charlotte Brontë

Note that you may or may not have to [Cap] each new line of dialogue. I have left these tags in just in case but I found I didn't always need them. Also, this drill is a little longer than the previous ones...you've been warned!

"[Open Quote][Cap]It is a long way off,[Comma] sir. [Period] "[Close Quote] [New Line]

"[Open Quote][Cap]No matter—[Dash]a girl of your sense will not object to the voyage or the distance. [Period] "[Close Quote] [New Line]

"[Open Quote][Cap]Not the voyage,[Comma] but the distance:[Colon] and then the sea is a barrier—[Dash] "[Close Quote] [New Line]

"[Open Quote][Cap]From what,[Comma] Jane?[Question Mark] "[Close Quote] [New Line]

"[Open Quote][Cap]From England and from Thornfield:[Colon] and—[Dash] "[Close Quote][New Line]

"[Open Quote][Cap]Well?[Question Mark] "[Close Quote] [New Line]

"[Open Quote][Cap]From you,[Comma] sir. [Period] "[Close Quote] [New Line]

I said this almost involuntarily,[Comma] and,[Comma] with as little sanction of free will,[Comma] my tears gushed out.[Period] I did not cry so as to be heard,[Comma] however;[Semicolon] I avoided sobbing.[Period] The thought of [Cap]Mrs. O'Gall[Spell That] and [Cap]Bitternutt [Cap]Lodge struck cold to my heart;[Semicolon] and colder the thought of all the brine and foam,[Comma] destined,[Comma] as it seemed,[Comma] to rush between me and the master at whose side I now walked,[Comma] and coldest the remembrance of the wider ocean—[Dash]wealth,[Comma] caste,[Comma] custom intervened between me and what I naturally and inevitably loved.[Period] [New Line]

"[Open Quote][Cap]It is a long way, [Comma]"[Close Quote]I again said.[Period] [New Line]

"[Open Quote][Cap]It is,[Comma] to be sure;[Semicolon] and when you get to [Cap]Bitternutt [Cap]Lodge,[Comma] Connaught[Spell That],[Comma] Ireland,[Comma] I shall never see you again,[Comma] Jane:[Colon] that's morally certain.[Period] I never go over to Ireland,[Comma] not having myself much of a fancy for the country.[Period] We have been good friends,[Comma] Jane;[Semicolon] have we not? [Question Mark] "[Close Quote][New Line]

"[Open Quote][Cap]Yes,[Comma] sir. [Period]"[Close Quote][New Line]

"[Open Quote][Cap]And when friends are on the eve of separation,[Comma] they like to spend the little time that remains to them close to each other.[Period] Come! [Exclamation Mark] we'll talk over the voyage and the parting quietly half-[Hyphen]an-[Hyphen]hour or so,[Comma] while the stars enter into their shining life up in heaven yonder:[Colon] here is the chestnut tree:[Colon] here is the bench at its old roots.[Period]

Come,[Comma] we will sit there in peace to-[Hyphen]night,[Comma] though we should never more be destined to sit there together. [Period]"[Close Quote] He seated me and himself.[Period] [New Line]

"[Open Quote][Cap]It is a long way to Ireland,[Comma] Janet,[Comma] and I am sorry to send my little friend on such weary travels:[Colon] but if I can't do better,[Comma] how is it to be helped? [Question Mark] Are you anything akin to me,[Comma] do you think,[Comma] Jane? [Question Mark] "[Close Quote][Select Ireland][choose: 1][All Caps That][Undo That][Undo That][New Line]

I could risk no sort of answer by this time:[Colon] my heart was still.[Period] [New Line]

"[Open Quote] [Cap]Because,[Comma]"[Close Quote]he said,[Comma] "[Open Quote]I sometimes have a queer feeling with regard to you—[Dash]especially when you are near me,[Comma] as now:[Colon] it is as if I had a string somewhere under my left ribs,[Comma] tightly and inextricably knotted to a similar string situated in the corresponding quarter of your little frame.[Period] And if that boisterous [Cap]Channel,[Comma] and two [Space] hundred [Space] miles or so of land come broad between us,[Comma] I am afraid that cord of communion will be snapt[Spell That];[Semicolon] and then I've a nervous notion I should take to bleeding inwardly.[Period] As for you, [Comma]—[Dash]you'd forget me. [Period]"[Close Quote][New Line]

"[Open Quote] [Cap]That I *never*[Italicize That] should,[Comma] sir:[Colon] you know—[Dash]"[Close Quote] [Cap]Impossible to proceed.[Period] [New Line]

"[Open Quote] [Cap]Jane,[Comma] do you hear that nightingale singing in the wood?[Question Mark] Listen![Exclamation Mark]"[Close Quote][New Line]

[Cap}In listening,[Comma] I sobbed convulsively;[Semicolon] for I could repress what I endured no longer;[Semicolon] I was obliged to yield,[Comma] and I was shaken from head to foot with acute distress.[Period] When I did speak,[Comma] it was only to express an impetuous wish that I had never been born,[Comma] or never come to [Cap]Thornfield.[Period] [New Line]

"[Open Quote][Cap]Because you are sorry to leave it?[Question Mark] "[Close Quote][New Line]

[Cap]The vehemence of emotion,[Comma] stirred by grief and love within me,[Comma] was claiming mastery,[Comma] and struggling for full sway,[Comma] and asserting a right to predominate,[Comma] to overcome,[Comma] to live,[Comma] rise,[Comma] and reign a long t last:[Colon] yes, [Comma]—[Dash]and to speak.[Period] [New Line]

"[Open Quote][Cap]I grieve to leave [Cap]Thornfield: [Colon] I love [Cap]Thornfield: [Colon] —[Dash]I love it,[Comma] because I have lived in it a full and delightful life, [Comma]—[Dash]momentarily at least.[Period] I have not been trampled on.[Period] I have not been petrified.[Period] I have not been buried with inferior minds,[Comma] and excluded from every glimpse of communion with what is bright and energetic and high.[Period] I have talked,[Comma] face to face,[Comma] with what I reverence,[Comma] with what I delight in, [Comma]—[Dash]with an original,[Comma] a vigorous,[Comma] an expanded mind.[Period] I have known you,[Comma] Mr. Rochester; [Semicolon] and it strikes me with terror and anguish to feel I absolutely must be torn from you for [Space] ever.[Period] I see the necessity of departure;[Semicolon] and it is like looking on the necessity of death.[Period]"[Close Quote][New Line]

"[Open Quote][Cap]Where do you see the necessity? [Question Mark] "[Close Quote]he asked suddenly.[Period] [New Line]

"[Open Quote][Cap]Where? [Question Mark] You,[Comma] sir,[Comma] have placed it before me.[Period]"[Close Quote][New Line]

"[Open Quote][Cap]In what shape? [Question Mark] "[Close Quote][New Line]

"[Open Quote][Cap]In the shape of Miss Ingram;[Semicolon] a noble and beautiful woman, [Comma]—[Dash]your bride. [Period]"[Close Quote][New Line]

"[Open Quote][Cap]My bride![Exclamation Mark] What bride?[Question Mark] I have no bride![Exclamation Mark]"[Close Quote][New Line]

"[Open Quote][Cap]But you will have. [Period]"[Close Quote][New Line]

"[Open Quote][Cap]Yes; [Semicolon]—[Dash]I will! [Exclamation Mark]—[Dash]I will![Exclamation Mark]"[Close Quote] He set his teeth.[Period] [New Line]

"[Open Quote][Cap]Then I must go: [Colon]—[Dash]you have said it yourself. [Period]"[Close Quote][New Line]

"[Open Quote][Cap]No:[Colon] you must stay! [Exclamation Mark] I swear it—[Dash]and the oath shall be kept.[Period]"[Close Quote][New Line]

"[Open Quote] [Cap]I tell you I must go! [Exclamation Mark]"[Close Quote]I retorted,[Comma] roused to something like passion.[Period] "[Open Quote]Do you think I can stay to become nothing to you?[Question Mark] Do you think I am an automaton?[Question Mark] —[Dash]a machine without feelings?[Question Mark] and can bear to have my morsel of bread snatched from my lips,[Comma] and my drop of living water dashed from my cup?[Question Mark] Do you think,[Comma] because I am poor,[Comma] obscure,[Comma] plain,[Comma] and little,[Comma] I am soulless and heartless? [Question Mark] You think wrong![Exclamation Mark]—[Dash]I have as much soul as you, [Comma]—[Dash]and full as much heart! [Exclamation Mark] And if God had gifted me with some beauty and much wealth,[Comma] I should have made it as hard for you to leave me,[Comma] as it is now for me to leave you.[Period] I am not talking to you now through the medium of custom,[Comma] conventionalities,[Comma] nor even of mortal flesh; [Semicolon]—[Dash]it is my spirit that addresses your spirit;[Semicolon] just as if both had passed through the grave,[Comma] and we stood at God's feet,[Comma] equal,[Comma]—[Dash]as we are![Exclamation Mark]"[Close Quote][New Line]

"[Open Quote][Cap]As we are![Exclamation Mark]"[Close Quote]repeated Mr. Rochester— [Dash]"[Open Quote][Close Quote][Open Quote]so, [Comma]"[Close Quote]he added,[Comma] enclosing me in his arms.[Period] Gathering me to his breast,[Comma] pressing his lips on my lips: "[Open Quote]so,[Comma] Jane! [Exclamation Mark]"[Close Quote][New Line]

"[Open Quote] [Cap]Yes,[Comma] so,[Comma] sir, [Comma]"[Close Quote]I rejoined:[Colon] "[Open

Quote]and yet not so;[Semicolon] for you are a married man—[Dash]or as good as a married man,[Comma] and wed to one inferior to you—[Dash]to one with whom you have no sympathy—[Dash]whom I do not believe you truly love;[Semicolon] for I have seen and heard you sneer at her.[Period] I would scorn such a union:[Colon] therefore I am better than you—[Dash]let me go![Exclamation Mark]"[Close Quote][New Line]

"[Open Quote] [Cap]Where,[Comma] Jane? [Question Mark] To Ireland? [Question Mark] "[Close Quote][New Line]

"[Open Quote] [Cap]Yes—[Dash]to Ireland.[Period] I have spoken my mind,[Comma] and can go anywhere now. [Period]"[Close Quote][New Line]

"[Open Quote] [Cap]Jane,[Comma] be still;[Semicolon] don't struggle so,[Comma] like a wild frantic bird that is rending its own plumage in its desperation.[Period]"[Close Quote][New Line]

"[Open Quote][Cap]I am no bird;[Semicolon] and no net ensnares me;[Semicolon] I am a free human being with an independent will,[Comma] which I now exert to leave you.[Period]"[Close Quote][New Line]

Practice Excerpt 4 without Prompts from Jane Eyre by Charlotte Brontë

"It is a long way off, sir."

"No matter—a girl of your sense will not object to the voyage or the distance."

"Not the voyage, but the distance: and then the sea is a barrier—"

"From what, Jane?"

"From England and from Thornfield: and—"

"Well?"

"From *you*, sir."

I said this almost involuntarily, and, with as little sanction of free will, my tears gushed out. I did not cry so as to be heard, however; I avoided sobbing. The thought of Mrs. O'Gall and Bitternutt Lodge struck cold to my heart; and colder the thought of all the brine and foam, destined, as it seemed, to rush between me and the master at whose side I now walked, and coldest the remembrance of the wider ocean—wealth, caste, custom intervened between me and what I naturally and inevitably loved.

"It is a long way," I again said.

"It is, to be sure; and when you get to Bitternutt Lodge, Connaught, Ireland, I shall never see you again, Jane: that's morally certain. I never go over to Ireland, not having myself much of a fancy for the country. We have been good friends, Jane; have we not?"

"Yes, sir."

"And when friends are on the eve of separation, they like to spend the little time that remains to them close to each other. Come! we'll talk over the voyage and the parting quietly half-an-hour or so, while the stars enter into their shining life up in heaven yonder: here is the chestnut tree: here is the bench at its old roots. Come, we will sit there in peace to-night, though we should never more be destined to sit there together." He seated me and himself.

"It is a long way to Ireland, Janet, and I am sorry to send my little friend on such weary travels: but if I can't do better, how is it to be helped? Are you anything akin to me, do you think, Jane?"

I could risk no sort of answer by this time: my heart was still.

"Because," he said, "I sometimes have a queer feeling with regard to you—especially when you are near me, as now: it is as if I had a string somewhere under my left ribs, tightly and inextricably knotted to a similar string situated in the corresponding quarter of your little frame. And if that boisterous Channel, and two hundred miles or so of land come broad between us, I am afraid that cord of communion will be snapt; and then I've a nervous notion I should take to bleeding inwardly. As for you,—you'd forget me."

"That I *never* should, sir: you know—" Impossible to proceed.

"Jane, do you hear that nightingale singing in the wood? Listen!"

In listening, I sobbed convulsively; for I could repress what I endured no longer; I was obliged to yield, and I was shaken from head to foot with acute distress. When I did speak, it was only to express an impetuous wish that I had never been born, or never come to Thornfield.

"Because you are sorry to leave it?"

The vehemence of emotion, stirred by grief and love within me, was claiming mastery, and struggling for full sway, and asserting a right to predominate, to overcome, to live, rise, and reign at last: yes,—and to speak.

"I grieve to leave Thornfield: I love Thornfield:—I love it, because I have lived in it a full and delightful life,—momentarily at least. I have not been trampled on. I have not been petrified. I have not been buried with inferior minds, and excluded from every glimpse of communion with what is bright and energetic and high. I have talked, face to face, with what I reverence, with what I delight in,—with an original, a vigorous, an expanded mind. I have known you, Mr. Rochester; and it strikes me with terror and anguish to feel I absolutely must be torn from you for ever. I see the necessity of departure; and it is like looking on the necessity of death."

"Where do you see the necessity?" he asked suddenly.

"Where? You, sir, have placed it before me."

"In what shape?"

"In the shape of Miss Ingram; a noble and beautiful woman,—your bride."

"My bride! What bride? I have no bride!"

"But you will have."

"Yes;—I will!—I will!" He set his teeth.

"Then I must go:—you have said it yourself."

"No: you must stay! I swear it—and the oath shall be kept."

"I tell you I must go!" I retorted, roused to something like passion. "Do you think I can stay to become nothing to you? Do you think I am an automaton?—a machine without feelings? and can bear to have my morsel of bread snatched from my lips, and my drop of living water dashed from my cup? Do you think, because I am poor, obscure, plain, and little, I am soulless and heartless? You think wrong!—I have as much soul as you,—and full as much heart! And if God had gifted me with some beauty and much wealth, I should have made it as hard for you to leave me, as it is now for me to leave you. I am not talking to you now through the medium of custom, conventionalities, nor even of mortal flesh;—it is my spirit that addresses your spirit; just as if both had passed through the grave, and we stood at God's feet, equal,—as we are!"

"As we are!" repeated Mr. Rochester—"so," he added, enclosing me in his arms. Gathering me to his breast, pressing his lips on my lips: "so, Jane!"

"Yes, so, sir," I rejoined: "and yet not so; for you are a married man—or as good as a married man, and wed to one inferior to you—to one with whom you have no sympathy—whom I do not believe you truly love; for I have seen and heard you sneer at her. I would scorn such a union: therefore I am better than you—let me go!"

"Where, Jane? To Ireland?"

"Yes—to Ireland. I have spoken my mind, and can go anywhere now."

"Jane, be still; don't struggle so, like a wild frantic bird that is rending its own plumage in its desperation."

"I am no bird; and no net ensnares me; I am a free human being with an independent will, which I now exert to leave you."

Next step: Dictate 2,000 words in your work in progress.

Dictation Drill 5: Navigation Commands

"Luck is the residue of design."

— John Milton

Objective: To become more proficient in navigating a document while dictating.

Your novel is an account that will inspire generations to come and improve civilization as we know it; however, it can feel like a mine field to navigate with dictation commands. This may be going too far for many novice dictationists, but I want you to be exposed to the commands.

Go to top

Go to bottom

Move down 6 lines

Go to beginning of line

Go to end of line

Go back

Press Enter

New line

Add space

Insert before [SAY A WORD IN YOUR PARAGRAPHS]

Move left 3 characters

Page down

Page up

Move right 10 characters

New Line

New paragraph

Press Enter

Insert after [SAY A WORD IN YOUR PARAGRAPHS]

Press Tab key

Tab 2 times

Go to End of Line

Go to beginning of line

Tab three times

Page Up

Go to Bottom

Go to Top

Page Down

New Line

New Paragraph

Add Line

Practice Excerpt 5 with Prompts: Pride and Prejudice by Jane Austen

I feel you should not use [Tab] for paragraph indents but instead just format paragraphs for the whole document, but in this drill I've included them so you can practice.

Remember, do not agonize about spelling variations or antiquated words.

[Tab][Cap]Mr. [Cap]Bingley[Spell That] was good-[Hyphen] looking and gentlemanlike;[Semicolon] he had a pleasant countenance,[Comma] and easy,[Comma] unaffected manners.[Period] [Go to Top, Go to Bottom] His sisters were fine women,[Comma] with an air of decided fashion.[Period] His brother- [Hyphen] in-[Hyphen] law,[Comma] [Cap]Mr. [Cap] Hurst,[Comma] merely looked the gentleman;[Semicolon] but his friend [Cap]Mr. [Cap]Darcy soon drew the attention of the room by his fine,[Comma] tall person,[Comma] handsome features,[Comma] noble mien[Spell That],[Comma] and the report which was in general circulation within five minutes after his entrance,[Comma] of his having ten thousand[Spell That] a year.[Period] The gentlemen pronounced him to be a fine figure of a man,[Comma] the ladies declared he was much handsomer than Mr. Bingley,[Comma] and he was looked at with great admiration for about half the evening,[Comma] till his manners gave a disgust which turned the tide of his popularity;[Semicolon] for he was discovered to be proud;[Semicolon] to be above his company, [Comma] and above being pleased;[Semicolon] and not all his large estate in [Cap]Derbyshire [Spell That] could then save him from having a most forbidding,[Comma] disagreeable countenance,[Comma] and being unworthy to be compared with his friend.[Period] [Go to Beginning of Line][Go to End of Line]. [Move Up Four Lines] then [Move Down Four Lines] [New Line]

[Tab] [Cap]Mr. Bingley had soon made himself acquainted with all the principal people in the room;[Semicolon] he was lively and unreserved,[Comma] danced every dance,[Comma] was angry that the ball closed so early,[Comma] and talked of giving one himself at [Cap]Netherfield[Spell That].[Period] Such amiable qualities must speak for themselves.[Period] What a contrast between him and his friend! [Exclamation Mark] [Cap]Mr. [Cap]Darcy danced only once with [Cap]Mrs. [Cap]Hurst and once with [Cap]Miss [Cap]Bingley,[Comma] declined being introduced to any other lady,[Comma] and spent the rest of the evening in walking about the room,[Comma] speaking occasionally to one of his own party.[Period] His character was decided.[Period] He was the proudest,[Comma] most disagreeable man in the world,[Comma] and everybody hoped that he would never come there again.[Period] Amongst the most violent against him was [Cap]Mrs. [Cap]Bennet[Spell That],[Comma] whose dislike of his general behaviour was sharpened into particular resentment by his having slighted one of her daughters.[Period] [Go to Beginning of Paragraph] [Go to End of Paragraph] [New Line]

[Tab][Cap]Elizabeth [Cap]Bennet had been obliged,[Comma] by the scarcity of gentlemen,[Comma] to sit down for two dances;[Semicolon] and during part of that time,[Comma] [Cap]Mr. [Cap]Darcy had been standing near enough for her to hear a conversation between him and [Cap]Mr. [Cap]Bingley,[Comma] who came from the dance for a few minutes,[Comma] to press his friend to join it.[Period][New Line]

[Tab]"[Open Quote] [Cap]Come,[Comma] Darcy,[Comma]" [Close Quote] said he,[Comma] "[Open Quote]I must have you dance.[Period] I hate to see you standing about by yourself in this stupid manner.[Period] You had much better dance.[Period]"[Close Quote][New Line]

[Tab] "[Open Quote] [Cap]I certainly shall not.[Period] You know how I detest it,[Comma] unless I am particularly acquainted with my partner.[Period] At such an assembly as this it would be insupportable.[Period] Your sisters are engaged,[Comma] and there is not another woman in the room whom it would not be a punishment to me to stand up with.[Period]"[Close Quote][New Line]

[Tab]"[Open Quote]I would not be so fastidious as you are,[Comma]"[Open Quote] cried [Cap]Mr. [Cap]Bingley,[Comma] "[Open Quote]for a kingdom![Exclamation Mark] Upon my honour,[Comma] I never met with so many pleasant girls in my life as I have this evening;[Semicolon] and there are several of them you see uncommonly pretty.[Period]"[Close Quote][New Line]

[Tab]"[Open Quote] [Cap]*You*[Italicize That] are dancing with the only handsome girl in the room,[Comma]"[Close Quote] said [Cap]Mr. [Cap]Darcy,[Comma] looking at the eldest [Cap]Miss [Cap]Bennet.[Period] [New Line]

[Tab] "[Open Quote]Oh! [Exclamation Mark] She is the most beautiful creature I ever beheld! [Exclamation

Mark] But there is one of her sisters sitting down just behind you,[Comma] who is very pretty,[Comma] and I dare say very agreeable.[Period] Do let me ask my partner to introduce you.[Period]"[Close Quote] [New Line]

[Tab]"[Open Quote] [Cap]Which do you mean?[Question Mark]"[Close Quote] and turning round he looked for a moment at Elizabeth,[Comma] till catching her eye,[Comma] he withdrew his own and coldly said:[Colon] "[Open Quote][Cap]She is tolerable,[Comma] but not handsome enough to tempt *me*;[Semicolon] I am in no humour at present to give consequence to young ladies who are slighted by other men.[Period] You had better return to your partner and enjoy her smiles,[Comma] for you are wasting your time with me.[Period]" [Close Quote][New Line]

[Tab] [Cap]Mr. [Cap]Bingley followed his advice.[Period] Mr. Darcy walked off;[Semicolon] and Elizabeth remained with no very cordial feelings toward him.[Period] She told the story,[Comma] however,[Comma] with great spirit among her friends;[Semicolon] for she had a lively,[Comma] playful disposition,[Comma] which delighted in anything ridiculous.[Period] [Go to Top] [Go to Bottom]

Practice Excerpt 5 without Prompts: Pride and Prejudice by Jane Austen

Mr. Bingley was good-looking and gentlemanlike; he had a pleasant countenance, and easy, unaffected manners. His sisters were fine women, with an air of decided fashion. His brother-in-law, Mr. Hurst, merely looked the gentleman; but his friend Mr. Darcy soon drew the attention of the room by his fine, tall person, handsome features, noble mien, and the report which was in general circulation within five minutes after his entrance, of his having ten thousand a year. The gentlemen pronounced him to be a fine figure of a man, the ladies declared he was much handsomer than Mr. Bingley, and he was looked at with great admiration for about half the evening, till his manners gave a disgust which turned the tide of his popularity; for he was discovered to be proud; to be above his company, and above being pleased; and not all his large estate in Derbyshire could then save him from having a most forbidding, disagreeable countenance, and being unworthy to be compared with his friend.

Mr. Bingley had soon made himself acquainted with all the principal people in the room; he was lively and unreserved, danced every dance, was angry that the ball closed so early, and talked of giving one himself at Netherfield. Such amiable qualities must speak for themselves. What a contrast between him and his friend! Mr. Darcy danced only once with Mrs. Hurst and once with Miss Bingley, declined being introduced to any other lady, and spent the rest of the evening in walking about the room, speaking occasionally to one of his own party. His character was decided. He was the proudest, most disagreeable man in the world, and everybody hoped that he would never come there again. Amongst the most violent against him was Mrs. Bennet, whose dislike of   the his general behaviour was sharpened into particular resentment by his having slighted one of her daughters.

Elizabeth Bennet had been obliged, by the scarcity of gentlemen, to sit down for two dances; and during part of that time, Mr. Darcy had been standing near enough for her to hear a conversation between him and Mr. Bingley, who came from the dance for a few minutes, to press his friend to join it.

"Come, Darcy," said he, "I must have you dance. I hate to see you standing about by yourself in this stupid manner. You had much better dance."

"I certainly shall not. You know how I detest it, unless I am particularly acquainted with my partner. At such an assembly as this it would be insupportable. Your sisters are engaged, and there is not another woman in the room whom it would not be a punishment to me to stand up with."

"I would not be so fastidious as you are," cried Mr. Bingley, "for a kingdom! Upon my honour, I never met with so many pleasant girls in my life as I have this evening; and there are several of them you see uncommonly pretty."

"*You* are dancing with the only handsome girl in the room," said Mr. Darcy, looking at the eldest Miss Bennet.

"Oh! She is the most beautiful creature I ever beheld! But there is one of her sisters sitting down just behind you, who is very pretty, and I dare say very agreeable. Do let me ask my partner to introduce you."

"Which do you mean?" and turning round he looked for a moment at Elizabeth, till catching her eye, he withdrew his own and coldly said: "She is tolerable, but not handsome enough to tempt *me*; I am in no humour at present to give consequence to young ladies who are slighted by other men. You had better return to your partner and enjoy her smiles, for you are wasting your time with me."

Mr. Bingley followed his advice. Mr. Darcy walked off; and Elizabeth remained with no very cordial feelings toward him. She told the story, however, with great spirit among her friends; for she had a lively, playful disposition, which delighted in anything ridiculous.

Next step: Dictate 2,000 words in your work in progress.

Dictation Drill 6: How to Revise with Text Editing Dictation Commands

"Truth, like gold, is to be obtained not by its growth, but by the washing away from it all that is not gold."

— Leo Tolstoy

Objective: To become more adept at dictating edits and corrections within a document.

You can do corrections as you go or after the fact by combining selection and editing commands.

1. Keep in mind that it can be ineffective to focus on editing when you are drafting.

2. That said, sometimes it all just gets too confusing if you don't make certain minor adjustments as you go.

Open a document with some text you can play with, and say the following.

Backspace

Undo that

Backspace 3

Undo that

the Delete lineand

Undo that

Delete last 4 words

Undo that

Backspace 10

Undo that

Redo that

Undo that

Select line

Cut that

Paste that

Select Paragraph

Delete It

Undo that

Select All

Delete It

Undo that

Delete last word

Undo that

Backspace 4

Undo that

Select previous paragraph

Delete that

Undo that

Practice Excerpt 6 with Prompts: From Frankenstein by Mary Shelley

Your software may use a different spelling than Shelley did, but rather than use [Spell That] like you might in real life, we're going to have some fun with it and use correction commands to change these to similar words.

You'll also notice I've stopped using so many [Cap] tags because the software figures it out, based on how well the sound and setup is working.

I trembled and my heart failed within me,[Comma] when,[Comma] on looking up,[Comma] I saw by the light of the moon the daemon at the casement.[Period] A ghastly grin wrinkled his lips as he gazed on me,[Comma] where I sat fulfilling the task which he had allotted to me.[Period] Yes,[Comma] he had followed me in my travels;[Semicolon] he had loitered in forests,[Comma] hid himself in caves,[Comma] or taken refuge in wide and desert heaths;[Semicolon] and he now came to mark my progress and claim the fulfilment of my promise.[Period] [New Line]

As I looked on him,[Comma] his countenance expressed the utmost extent of malice and treachery.[Period] I thought with a sensation of madness on my promise of creating another like to him,[Comma] and trembling with passion,[Comma] tore to pieces the thing on which I was engaged.[Period] The wretch saw me destroy the creature on whose future existence he depended for happiness,[Comma] and with a howl of devilish despair and revenge,[Comma] withdrew.[Period] [New Line]

I left the room,[Comma] and locking the door,[Comma] made a solemn vow in my own heart never to resume my labours [Backspace 7] work;[Semicolon] and then,[Comma] with trembling steps,[Comma] I sought my own apartment.[Period] I was alone;[Semicolon] none were near me to dissipate the gloom and relieve me from the sickening oppression of the most terrible reveries[Undo That][Redo That].[Period] [New Line]

Several hours passed,[Comma] and I remained near my window gazing on the sea;[Semicolon] it was almost motionless,[Comma] for the winds were hushed,[Comma] and all nature reposed under the eye of the quiet moon.[Period] A few fishing vessels alone specked the water,[Comma] and now and then the gentle breeze wafted the sound of voices as the fishermen called to one another.[Period] I felt the silence,[Comma] although I was hardly conscious of its extreme profundity,[Comma] until my ear was suddenly arrested by the paddling of oars near the shore,[Comma] and a person landed close to my house.[Period] [New Line]

[Cap]In a few minutes after,[Comma] I heard the creaking of my door,[Comma] as if some one [backspace 3] person endeavoured[Delete That] tried to open it softly.[Period] I trembled from head to foot;[Semicolon] I felt a presentiment of who it was and wished to rouse one of the peasants who dwelt in a cottage not far from mine;[Semicolon] but I was overcome by the sensation of helplessness,[Comma] so often felt in frightful dreams,[Comma] when you in vain endeavor[undo that] ambition to fly from an impending danger,[Comma] and was rooted to the spot.[Period] Presently I heard the sound of footsteps[Undo That] [Redo That] along the passage;[Semicolon] the door opened,[Comma] and the wretch whom I dreaded appeared.[Period] [New Line]

[Cap]Shutting the door,[Comma] he approached me and said in a smothered voice,[Comma] "[Open Quote]You have destroyed the work which you began;[Semicolon] what is it that you intend? [Question Mark] Do you dare to break your promise? [Question Mark] I have endured toil and misery;[Semicolon] I left Switzerland with you;[Semicolon] I crept along the shores of the Rhine,[Comma] among its willow islands and over the summits of its hills.[Period] I have dwelt many months[Undo That][Redo That] in the heaths of England and among the deserts of Scotland.[Period] I have endured incalculable fatigue,[Comma] and cold,[Comma] and hunger;[Semicolon] do you dare destroy my hopes? [Question Mark] "[Close Quote] [New Line]

"[Open Quote]Begone! [Exclamation Mark] I do break my promise;[Semicolon] never will I create another like yourself,[Comma] equal in deformity and wickedness. [Period]"[Close Quote] [New Line]

"[Open Quote]Slave,[Comma] I before reasoned with you,[Comma] but you have proved yourself unworthy of my condescension.[Period] Remember that I have power;[Semicolon] you believe yourself miserable,[Comma] but I can make you so wretched that the light of day will be hateful to you.[Period] You are my creator,[Comma] but I am your master;[Semicolon] obey! [Exclamation Mark]"[Close Quote] [New Line]

"[Open Quote]The hour of my irresolution is past,[Comma] and the period of your power is arrived.[Period] Your threats cannot move me to do an act of wickedness;[Semicolon] but they confirm me in a determination of not creating you a companion in vice.[Period] Shall I,[Comma] in cool blood,[Comma] set loose upon the earth a daemon whose delight is in death and wretchedness? [Question Mark] Begone! [Exclamation Mark] I am firm,[Comma] and your words will only exasperate my rage. [Period]"[Close Quote] [New Line]

The monster saw my determination in my face and gnashed his teeth in the impotence of anger.[Period] "[Open Quote]Shall each man, [Comma]"[Open Quote] cried he,[Comma] "[Open Quote]find a wife for his bosom,[Comma] and each beast have his mate,[Comma] and I be alone? [Question Mark] I had feelings of affection, [Comma] and they were requited by detestation and scorn[Undo That] [Redo That].[Period] Man![Exclamation Mark] You may hate,[Comma] but beware! [Exclamation Mark] Your hours will pass in dread and misery,[Comma] and soon the bolt will fall which must ravish from you your happiness forever.[Period] Are you to be happy while I grovel in the intensity of my wretchedness? [Question Mark] You can blast my other passions,[Comma] but revenge remains— [Dash]revenge,[Comma] henceforth dearer than light or food! [Exclamation Mark] I may die,[Comma] but first you,[Comma] my tyrant and tormentor,[Comma] shall curse the sun that gazes on your misery.[Period] Beware,[Comma] for I am fearless and therefore powerful.[Period] I will watch with the wiliness of a snake,[Comma] that I may sting with its venom.[Period] Man,[Comma] you shall repent of the injuries you inflict. [Period]"[Close Quote]

Practice Excerpt 6 without Prompts: From Frankenstein by Mary Shelley

Your software may use a different spelling than Shelley did, so you will need to use correction commands to preserve her spelling.

I trembled and my heart failed within me, when, on looking up, I saw by the light of the moon the daemon at the casement. A ghastly grin wrinkled his lips as he gazed on me, where I sat fulfilling the task which he had allotted to me. Yes, he had followed me in my travels; he had loitered in forests, hid himself in caves, or taken refuge in wide and desert heaths; and he now came to mark my progress and claim the fulfilment of my promise.

As I looked on him, his countenance expressed the utmost extent of malice and treachery. I thought with a sensation of madness on my promise of creating another like to him, and trembling with passion, tore to pieces the thing on which I was engaged. The wretch saw me destroy the creature on whose future existence he depended for happiness, and with a howl of devilish despair and revenge, withdrew.

I left the room, and locking the door, made a solemn vow in my own heart never to resume my labours; and then, with trembling steps, I sought my own apartment. I was alone; none were near me to dissipate the gloom and relieve me from the sickening oppression of the most terrible reveries.

Several hours passed, and I remained near my window gazing on the sea; it was almost motionless, for the winds were hushed, and all nature reposed under the eye of the quiet moon. A few fishing vessels alone specked the water, and now and then the gentle breeze wafted the sound of voices as the fishermen called to one another. I felt the silence, although I was hardly conscious of its extreme profundity, until my ear was suddenly arrested by the paddling of oars near the shore, and a person landed close to my house.

In a few minutes after, I heard the creaking of my door, as if some one endeavoured to open it softly. I trembled from head to foot; I felt a presentiment of who it was and wished to rouse one of the peasants who dwelt in a cottage not far from mine; but I was overcome by the sensation of helplessness, so often felt in frightful dreams, when you in vain endeavour to fly from an impending danger, and was rooted to the spot. Presently I heard the sound of footsteps along the passage; the door opened, and the wretch whom I dreaded appeared.

Shutting the door, he approached me and said in a smothered voice, "You have destroyed the work which you began; what is it that you intend? Do you dare to break your promise? I have endured toil and misery; I left Switzerland with you; I crept along the shores of the Rhine, among its willow islands and over the summits of its hills. I have dwelt many months in the heaths of England and among the deserts of Scotland. I have endured incalculable fatigue, and cold, and hunger; do you dare destroy my hopes?"

"Begone! I do break my promise; never will I create another like yourself, equal in deformity and wickedness."

"Slave, I before reasoned with you, but you have proved yourself unworthy of my condescension. Remember that I have power; you believe yourself miserable, but I can make you so wretched that the light of day will be hateful to you. You are my creator, but I am your master; obey!"

"The hour of my irresolution is past, and the period of your power is arrived. Your threats cannot move me to do an act of wickedness; but they confirm me in a determination of not creating you a companion in vice. Shall I, in cool blood, set loose upon the earth a daemon whose delight is in death and wretchedness? Begone! I am firm, and your words will only exasperate my rage."

The monster saw my determination in my face and gnashed his teeth in the impotence of anger. "Shall each man," cried he, "find a wife for his bosom, and each beast have his mate, and I be alone? I had feelings of affection, and they were requited by detestation and scorn. Man! You may hate, but beware! Your hours will pass in dread and misery, and soon the bolt will fall which must ravish from you your happiness forever. Are you to be happy while I grovel in the intensity of my wretchedness? You can blast my other passions, but revenge remains— revenge, henceforth dearer than light or food! I may die, but first you, my tyrant and tormentor, shall curse the sun that gazes on your misery. Beware, for I am fearless and therefore powerful. I will watch with the wiliness of a snake, that I may sting with its venom. Man, you shall repent of the injuries you inflict."

Next step: Dictate 2,000 words in your work in progress.

Dictation Drill 7: Text Formatting Commands

"Man is a mystery. It needs to be unravelled, and if you spend your whole life unravelling it, don't say that you've wasted time. I am studying that mystery because I want to be a human being."

— Fyodor Dostoyevsky

Objective: To become more adept at dictating text formatting within a document.

Similar to the last drill, formatting text really shouldn't be your primary concern while getting a draft out, in my opinion, but sometimes it does keep things more clear.

Try some of these selection and formatting commands.

Select sentence

Italicize that

Select paragraph

Bold that

Select previous word

Underline that

Select next word

Sct Word to strikeout

Select All

Increase Font to 36 points

Set Font to Times New Roman

Decrease Font to 12 points

Decrease Font

Decrease Font

Increase Font

Increase Font

Format that regular

Select All

Set Font Color to Pink

Format that regular

Select previous word

Italicize That

Undo That

Practice Excerpt 7 with Prompts: From The Fall of the House of Usher by Edgar Allan Poe

[Set font to Times New Roman]I have said that the sole effect of my somewhat childish experiment—[Dash]that of looking down within the tarn[Spell That]—[Dash]had been to deepen the first singular impression.[Period] There can be no doubt that the consciousness of the rapid increase of my superstition—[Dash]for why should I not so term it? [Question Mark] —[Dash]served mainly to accelerate the increase itself.[Period] Such,[Comma] I have long known,[Comma] is the paradoxical law of all sentiments having terror as a basis.[Period] And it might have been for this reason only,[Comma] that,[Comma] when I again uplifted my eyes to the house itself,[Comma] from its image in the pool,[Comma] there grew in my mind a strange fancy—[Dash]a fancy so ridiculous,[Comma] indeed,[Comma] that I but mention it to show the vivid force of the sensations which oppressed me.[Period] I had so worked upon my imagination as really to believe that about the whole mansion and domain there hung an atmosphere peculiar to themselves and their immediate vicinity—[Dash]an atmosphere which had no affinity with the air of heaven,[Comma] but which had reeked up from the decayed trees,[Comma] and the gray wall,[Comma] and the silent tarn—[Dash]a pestilent and mystic vapor,[Comma] dull,[Comma] sluggish,[Comma] faintly discernible,[Comma] and leaden-[Hyphen]hued.[Period] [Select Paragraph][Bold That][Italicize That][Undo That][Undo That][Set font to Arial][Unselect That][New Line]

Shaking off from my spirit what *must*[Italicize That] have been a dream,[Comma] I scanned more narrowly the real aspect of the building.[Period] Its principal feature seemed to be that of an excessive antiquity.[Period] The discoloration of ages had been great.[Period] Minute fungi overspread the whole exterior,[Comma] hanging in a fine tangled web-[Hyphen]work from the eaves.[Period] Yet all this was apart from any extraordinary dilapidation.[Period] No portion of the masonry had fallen;[Semicolon] and there appeared to be a wild inconsistency between its still perfect adaptation of parts,[Comma] and the crumbling condition of the individual stones.[Period] [Select Line] [Underline That] [Undo That][Unselect That] In this there was much that reminded me of the specious totality of old wood-[Hyphen]work which has rotted for long years in some neglected vault,[Comma] with no disturbance from the breath of the external air.[Period] [Select Sentence][Increase Font] [Increase Font] [Decrease Font] [Decrease Font] [Unselect That]Beyond this indication of extensive decay,[Comma] however,[Comma] the fabric gave little token of instability.[Period] Perhaps the eye of a scrutinizing observer might have discovered a barely perceptible fissure,[Comma] which,[Comma] extending from the roof of the building in front,[Comma] made its way down the wall in a zigzag direction,[Comma] until it became lost in the sullen waters of the tarn.[Period] [Select Last 3 Sentences] [Set Font to 36 Points][Format That Regular][Unselect That][New Line]

Noticing these things,[Comma] I rode over a short causeway to the house.[Period] A servant in waiting took my horse,[Comma] and I entered the Gothic archway of the hall. [Select All] [Bold That][Italicize That][Undo That][Undo That][Unselect That][New Line]

A valet,[Comma] of stealthy step,[Comma] thence conducted me,[Comma] in silence,[Comma] through many dark and intricate passages in my progress to the *studio*[Italicize That] of his master.[Period] Much that I encountered on the way contributed,[Comma] I know not how,[Comma] to heighten the vague sentiments of which I have already spoken.[Period] While the objects around me—while the carvings of the ceilings,[Comma] the sombre tapestries of the walls,[Comma] the ebon blackness of the floors,[Comma] and the phantasmagoric armorial trophies which rattled as I strode,[Comma] were but matters to which,[Comma] or to such as which,[Comma] I had been accustomed from my infancy—[Dash] while I hesitated not to acknowledge how familiar was all this—[Dash] I still wondered to find how unfamiliar were the fancies which ordinary images were stirring up.[Period] On one of the staircases,[Comma] I met the physician of the family.[Period] His countenance,[Comma] I thought,[Comma] wore a mingled expression of low cunning and perplexity.[Period] He accosted me with trepidation and passed on.[Period] The valet now threw open a door and ushered me into the presence of his master.[Period][New Line]

[Cap]The room in which I found myself was very large and lofty.[Period] The windows were long,[Comma] narrow,[Comma] and pointed,[Comma] and at so vast a distance from the black oaken floor as to be altogether inaccessible from within.[Period] Feeble gleams of encrimsoned light made their way through the trellised panes,[Comma] and served to render sufficiently distinct the more prominent objects around; [Semicolon] the eye,[Comma] however,[Comma] struggled in vain to reach the remoter angles of the chamber,[Comma] or the recesses of the vaulted and fretted ceiling.[Period] Dark draperies hung upon the walls.[Period] The general furniture was profuse,[Comma] comfortless,[Comma] antique,[Comma] and tattered.[Period] Many books and musical instruments lay scattered about,[Comma] but failed to give any vitality to the scene.[Period] I felt that I breathed an atmosphere of sorrow.[Period] An air of stern,[Comma] deep,[Comma] and irredeemable gloom hung over and pervaded all.[Period]

Practice Excerpt 7 without Prompts: From The Fall of the House of Usher by Edgar Allan Poe

I have said that the sole effect of my somewhat childish experiment—that of looking down within the tarn—had been to deepen the first singular impression. There can be no doubt that the consciousness of the rapid increase of my superstition—for why should I not so term it?—served mainly to accelerate the increase itself. Such, I have long known, is the paradoxical law of all sentiments having terror as a basis. And it might have been for this reason only, that, when I again uplifted my eyes to the house itself, from its image in the pool, there grew in my mind a strange fancy—a fancy so ridiculous, indeed, that I but mention it to show the vivid force of the sensations which oppressed me. I had so worked upon my imagination as really to believe that about the whole mansion and domain there hung an atmosphere peculiar to themselves and their immediate vicinity—an atmosphere which had no affinity with the air of heaven, but which had reeked up from the decayed trees, and the gray wall, and the silent tarn—a pestilent and mystic vapor, dull, sluggish, faintly discernible, and leaden-hued.

Shaking off from my spirit what *must* have been a dream, I scanned more narrowly the real aspect of the building. Its principal feature seemed to be that of an excessive antiquity. The discoloration of ages had been great. Minute fungi overspread the whole exterior, hanging in a fine tangled web-work from the eaves. Yet all this was apart from any extraordinary dilapidation. No portion of the masonry had fallen; and there appeared to be a wild inconsistency between its still perfect adaptation of parts, and the crumbling condition of the individual stones. In this there was much that reminded me of the specious totality of old wood-work which has rotted for long years in some neglected vault, with no disturbance from the breath of the external air. Beyond this indication of extensive decay, however, the fabric gave little token of instability. Perhaps the eye of a scrutinizing observer might have discovered a barely perceptible fissure, which, extending from the roof of the building in front, made its way down the wall in a zigzag direction, until it became lost in the sullen waters of the tarn.

Noticing these things, I rode over a short causeway to the house. A servant in waiting took my horse, and I entered the Gothic archway of the hall. A valet, of stealthy step, thence conducted me, in silence, through many dark and intricate passages in my progress to the *studio* of his master. Much that I encountered on the way contributed, I know not how, to heighten the vague sentiments of which I have already spoken. While the objects around me—while the carvings of the ceilings, the sombre tapestries of the walls, the ebon blackness of the floors, and the phantasmagoric armorial trophies which rattled as I strode, were but matters to which, or to such as which, I had been accustomed from my infancy—while I hesitated not to acknowledge how familiar was all this— I still wondered to find how unfamiliar were the fancies which ordinary images were stirring up. On one of the staircases, I met the physician of the family. His countenance, I thought, wore a mingled expression of low cunning and perplexity. He accosted me with trepidation and passed on. The valet now threw open a door and ushered me into the presence of his master.

The room in which I found myself was very large and lofty. The windows were long, narrow, and pointed, and at so vast a distance from the black oaken floor as to be altogether inaccessible from within. Feeble gleams of encrimsoned light made their way through the trellised panes, and served to render sufficiently distinct the more prominent objects around; the eye, however, struggled in vain to reach the remoter angles of the chamber, or the recesses of the vaulted and fretted ceiling. Dark draperies hung upon the walls. The general furniture was profuse, comfortless, antique, and tattered. Many books and musical instruments lay scattered about, but failed to give any vitality to the scene. I felt that I breathed an atmosphere of sorrow. An air of stern, deep, and irredeemable gloom hung over and pervaded all.

Done! Next step: Dictate 2,000 words in your work in progress.

Dictation Drill 8: Paragraph Formatting

"The mind is its own place, and in itself can make a heaven of hell, a hell of heaven."

— John Milton

Objective: To dictate paragraph formatting commands such as indents, tables, and alignment.

A lot of paragraph styling could be done after you are done with your draft, but it's worth going through these formatting commands just in case you need them.

Say the following:

Set the Paragraph to Bulleted

[TYPE YOUR FAVORITE COLOR]

New Line

[TYPE ANOTHER FAVORITE COLOR]

New Line

[TYPE ANOTHER FAVORITE COLOR]

Select Paragraph

Single Space

Double Space

Justify

Right Align

Center Align

Left Align

Select Next Line

Center Align

Right Align

Left Align

Set the Paragraph to Numbered

[TYPE YOUR FAVORITE FOOD]

Next Line

[TYPE YOUR FAVORITE FOOD]

Next Line

[TYPE YOUR FAVORITE FOOD]

Next Line

Next Line

Select previous paragraph

Set the paragraph to bulleted

Practice Excerpt 8 with Prompts: From Dracula by Bram Stoker

For this passage, practice both text and paragraph format commands to make the text look as close to the original as you can.

[Italicize That]Mina Harker's Journal. [Period][Center That] [New Line]

29 September.[Period][Italicize That]—[Dash]After I had tidied myself,[Comma] I went down to Dr.[Period] Seward's study.[Period] At the door I paused a moment,[Comma] for I thought I heard him talking with some one.[Period] As,[Comma] however,[Comma] he had pressed me to be quick,[Comma] I knocked at the door,[Comma] and on his calling out,[Comma] "[Open Quote]Come in, [Comma]"[Close Quote] I entered.[Period] [New Line]

To my intense surprise,[Comma] there was no one with him.[Period] He was quite alone,[Comma] and on the table opposite him was what I knew at once from the description to be a phonograph. [Period] I had never seen one,[Comma] and was much interested.[Period] [Select Paragraph] [Double Space][Single Space][Unselect Paragraph][New Line]

"[Open Quote]I hope I did not keep you waiting,[Comma]"[Close Quote]I said;[Semicolon] "[Open Quote]but I stayed at the door as I heard you talking,[Comma] and thought there was some one with you.[Period] "[Close Quote][Select Paragraph][Center That][Justify That][Undo That][Undo That[Unselect That]][New Line]

"[Open Quote]Oh, [Comma]"[Close Quote]he replied might be going crazy with a smile,[Comma] "[Open Quote]I was only entering my diary. [Period]"[Close Quote][New Line]

"[Open Quote]Your diary? [Question Mark] "[Close Quote]I asked him in surprise.[Period] [New Line]

"[Open Quote]Yes, [Comma]"[Close Quote]he answered.[Period] "[Open Quote]I keep it in this. [Period]"[Close Quote]As he spoke he laid his hand on the phonograph.[Period] I felt quite excited over it,[Comma] and blurted out: [Colon]—[Dash] [New Line]

"[Open Quote]Why,[Comma] this beats even shorthand! [Exclamation Mark] May I hear it say something? [Question Mark] "[Close Quote][New Line]

"[Open Quote]Certainly, [Comma]"[Close Quote]he replied with alacrity,[Comma] and stood up to put it in train for speaking.[Period] Then he paused,[Comma] and a troubled look overspread his face.[Period] [New Line]

"[Open Quote]The fact is, [Comma]"[Close Quote]he began awkwardly,[Comma] "[Open Quote]I only keep my diary in it;[Semicolon] and as it is entirely—[Dash]almost entirely—[Dash]about my cases,[Comma] it may be awkward—[Dash]that is,[Comma] I mean—[Dash]—[Dash]"[Close Quote]He stopped,[Comma] and I tried to help him out of his embarrassment: [Colon]—[Dash] [New Line]

"[Open Quote]You helped to attend dear Lucy at the end.[Period] Let me hear how she died;[Semicolon] for all that I know of her,[Comma] I shall be very grateful.[Period] She was very,[Comma] very dear to me.[Period]"[Close Quote][New Line]

To my surprise,[Comma] he answered,[Comma] with a horrorstruck look in his face: [Colon]—[Dash] [New Line]

"[Open Quote] [Cap]Tell you of her death? [Question Mark] Not for the wide world! [Exclamation Mark]"[Close Quote][New Line]

"[Open Quote]Why not? [Question Mark] "[Close Quote]I asked,[Comma] for some grave,[Comma] terrible feeling was coming over me.[Period] Again he paused,[Comma] and I could see that he was trying to invent an excuse.[Period] At length he stammered out: [Colon]—[Dash] [New Line]

"[Open Quote]You see,[Comma] I do not know how to pick out any particular part of the diary. [Period]"[Close Quote]Even while he was speaking an idea dawned upon him...[Elipsis][New Line]

Then it was terrible;[Semicolon] my intuition was right! [Exclamation Mark] For a moment I thought,[Comma] and as my eyes ranged the room,[Comma] unconsciously looking for something or some opportunity to aid me,[Comma] they lit on a great batch of typewriting on the table.[Period] His eyes caught the look in mine,[Comma] and,[Comma] without his thinking,[Comma] followed their direction.[Period] As they saw the parcel he realised my meaning.[Period] [New Line]

"[Open Quote] [Cap]You do not know me, [Comma]"[Close Quote]I said.[Period] "[Open Quote] [Cap]When you have read those papers—[Dash]my own diary and my husband's also,[Comma] which I have typed—[Dash]you will know me better.[Period] I have not faltered in giving every thought of my own heart in this cause;[Semicolon] but,[Comma] of course,[Comma] you do not know me—[Dash]yet;[Semicolon] and I must not expect you to trust me so far.[Period] "[Close Quote][Select Last Paragraph] [Set Paragraph to Bulleted][Undo That] [Set Paragraph to Numbered][Undo That][Unselect That][New Line]

He is certainly a man of noble nature; [Semicolon] poor dear Lucy was right about him.[Period] He stood up and opened a large drawer,[Comma] in which[Spell That] were arranged in order a number of hollow cylinders of metal covered with dark wax,[Comma] and said: [Colon]—[Dash] [New Line]

"[Open Quote]You are quite right.[Period] I did not trust you because I did not know you.[Period] But I know you now;[Semicolon] and let me say that I should have known you long ago.[Period] I know that Lucy told you of me;[Semicolon] she told me of you too.[Period] May I make the only atonement in my power? [Question Mark] Take the cylinders and hear them—[Dash]the first half-[Hyphen]dozen of them are personal to me,[Comma] and they will not horrify you;[Semicolon] then you will know me better.[Period] Dinner will by then be ready.[Period] In the meantime I shall read over some of these documents,[Comma] and shall be better able to understand certain things. [Period]"[Close Quote]He carried the phonograph himself up to my sitting-[Hyphen]room and adjusted it for me.[Period] Now I shall learn something pleasant,[Comma] I am sure;[Semicolon] for it will tell me the other side of a true love episode of which I know one side already... [Ellipsis] [New Line]

[Center That]Dr. Seward's Diary.[Period] [Italicize That][New Line]

29 September. [Period][Italicize That]—[Dash]I was so absorbed in that wonderful diary of Jonathan Harker and that other of his wife that I let the time run on without thinking.[Period] Mrs. Harker was not down when the maid came to announce dinner,[Comma] so I said:[Colon] "[Open Quote] She is possibly tired;[Semicolon] let dinner wait an hour,[Comma]"[Close Quote]and I went on with my work.[Period] I had just finished [Period] Harker's diary,[Comma] when she came in.[Period] She looked sweetly pretty,[Comma] but very sad,[Comma] and her eyes were flushed with crying.[Period] This somehow moved me much...[Ellipsis] [Select All] [Right Align That][Undo That][Justify That][Undo That][Unselect That]

Practice Excerpt 8 without Prompts: From Dracula by Bram Stoker

Mina Harker's Journal.

29 September.—After I had tidied myself, I went down to Dr. Seward's study. At the door I paused a moment, for I thought I heard him talking with some one. As, however, he had pressed me to be quick, I knocked at the door, and on his calling out, "Come in," I entered.

To my intense surprise, there was no one with him. He was quite alone, and on the table opposite him was what I knew at once from the description to be a phonograph. I had never seen one, and was much interested.

"I hope I did not keep you waiting," I said; "but I stayed at the door as I heard you talking, and thought there was some one with you."

"Oh," he replied with a smile, "I was only entering my diary."

"Your diary?" I asked him in surprise.

"Yes," he answered. "I keep it in this." As he spoke he laid his hand on the phonograph. I felt quite excited over it, and blurted out:—

"Why, this beats even shorthand! May I hear it say something?"

"Certainly," he replied with alacrity, and stood up to put it in train for speaking. Then he paused, and a troubled look overspread his face.

"The fact is," he began awkwardly, "I only keep my diary in it; and as it is entirely—almost entirely—

about my cases, it may be awkward—that is, I mean——" He stopped, and I tried to help him out of his embarrassment:—

"You helped to attend dear Lucy at the end. Let me hear how she died; for all that I know of her, I shall be very grateful. She was very, very dear to me."

To my surprise, he answered, with a horrorstruck look in his face:—

"Tell you of her death? Not for the wide world!"

"Why not?" I asked, for some grave, terrible feeling was coming over me. Again he paused, and I could see that he was trying to invent an excuse. At length he stammered out:—

"You see, I do not know how to pick out any particular part of the diary." Even while he was speaking an idea dawned upon him...

Then it was terrible; my intuition was right! For a moment I thought, and as my eyes ranged the room, unconsciously looking for something or some opportunity to aid me, they lit on a great batch of typewriting on the table. His eyes caught the look in mine, and, without his thinking, followed their direction. As they saw the parcel he realised my meaning.

"You do not know me," I said. "When you have read those papers—my own diary and my husband's also, which I have typed—you will know me better. I have not faltered in giving every thought of my own heart in this cause; but, of course, you do not know me— yet; and I must not expect you to trust me so far."

He is certainly a man of noble nature; poor dear Lucy was right about him. He stood up and opened a large drawer, in which were arranged in order a number of hollow cylinders of metal covered with dark wax, and said:—

"You are quite right. I did not trust you because I did not know you. But I know you now; and let me say that I should have known you long ago. I know that Lucy told you of me; she told me of you too. May I make the only atonement in my power? Take the cylinders and hear them—the first half-dozen of them are personal to me, and they will not horrify you; then you will know me better. Dinner will by then be ready. In the meantime I shall read over some of these documents, and shall be better able to understand certain things." He carried the phonograph himself up to my sitting-room and adjusted it for me. Now I shall learn something pleasant, I am sure; for it will tell me the other side of a true love episode of which I know one side already....

Dr. Seward's Diary.

29 September.—I was so absorbed in that wonderful diary of Jonathan Harker and that other of his wife that I let the time run on without thinking. Mrs. Harker was not down when the maid came to announce dinner, so I said: "She is possibly tired; let dinner wait an hour," and I went on with my work. I had just finished Mrs. Harker's diary, when she came in. She looked sweetly pretty, but very sad, and her eyes were flushed with crying. This somehow moved me much...

You're done! Next step: Dictate 2,000 words in your work in progress.

Dictation Drill 9: Stream of Consciousness

"I swear to you gentlemen, that to be overly conscious is a sickness, a real, thorough sickness."

"Talking nonsense is the sole privilege mankind possesses over the other organisms. It's by talking nonsense that one gets to the truth! I talk nonsense, therefore I'm human."

— Fyodor Dostoyevsky, Notes from Underground

Objective: To become more adept at speaking continuously without stopping, so that you think more fluidly in general while dictating.

As you move into the next stage, you'll be polishing verbal storytelling skills.

This next method could become your favorite go-to dictation practice drill. One of the first tools I learned for creative writing was in my junior high English class. My teacher asked us to warm up using a stream of consciousness exercise. Her requirement was that we not lift our pens from the paper. This meant that no matter what gibberish came out, we had to keep writing.

You can do the same thing with dictation.

1. If you stress out too much with this it really will be gibberish. But if you just keep going without forcing what to say next, you'll likely be surprised to find yourself thinking somewhat sensical and super creative phrases and sentences. The idea is that out of the page of

strangeness, a golden nugget just might be discovered – something your conscious writer mind might not have let you come up with.

2. It takes most people at least a minute or two to get into that zone.

3. As with brainstorming, don't edit or judge what you say.

4. You can decide whether punctuation is important or not. When I do stream of consciousness exercises, I use punctuation because I hardly think about it anymore and it doesn't distract me.

5. Have fun with it! Some of my favorite writing has come from stream of consciousness.

You're done! Next step: Dictate 2,500 words in your work in progress.

Dictation Drill 10: Reciting Something from Memory

"We cannot live better than in seeking to become better."

— Socrates

Objective: To become better at speaking ideas from memory.

In this drill, recite something you have memorized. If your mind goes blank, try song lyrics even if it's just a popular birthday song or something. Just don't sing the song, speak it! Other options: national anthems, school fight songs, nonsense songs you sing to your kids, holiday songs, or poetry. The point here is to now break away from reading a dictation.

If you need to, set a timer, but do this for about 15 minutes.

1. Include punctuation, capitalization, and new lines if you can.

2. Pay attention to speaking evenly and trying not to pause too long.

3. Since most songs or recitations we have memorized are likely to be on the shorter side, consider repeating the memorized content until you have practiced your allotted time.

You're done! Next step: Dictate 2,500 words in your work in progress.

Dictation Drill 11: Dictate a Brainstorm or List

"If you want to overcome the whole world, overcome yourself."

— *Fyodor Dostoyevsky, Demons*

Objective: To become more versed in dictation by vocalizing a list of items, rather than typing or writing them.

By practicing verbalizing lists for practical aspects of your life, you can also strengthen your dictation skills for creative projects like dictating your novel.

You could dictate a shopping list, to-do lists, project brainstorms, goal lists, food you want to make or eat, whatever. Just try to practice this steadily for 15 minutes.

1. Choose either Dragon for desktop, Dragon for mobile, or your device's voice assistant (Siri, Cortana, Now, etc) and open or activate the program if needed.

2. Dictate each item, saying New Line or the appropriate command for the system you are using.

3. If this is difficult, try coming up with a general on-going to-do list or grocery list or other shopping list, not just one for today or this week.

4. You could also try a free association such as speaking a word relating to your work in progress for every letter

of the alphabet. For example, for my story THE SALT SHEEN PARADOX I might list: Aviatrix, Beatrice (my main character), Charlie (her boss)...

Next step: Dictate 2,500 words in your work in progress.

Dictation Drill 12: Dictating Your Blog or Writer's Journal

"Granted, granted I'm a babbler, a harmless, irksome babbler, as we all are. But what's to be done if the sole and express purpose of every intelligent man is babble-- that is, a deliberate pouring from empty into void."

— Fyodor Dostoyevsky, Notes from Underground

Objective: To express your writing life via dictation rather than typing or writing.

Dictating about your writing life or process is a great way to strengthen your verbal storytelling ability as well.

1. If you have a blog, this is a great time to babble about something less research-oriented, like funny things about being a writer, your writing process, or anything else you can simply ramble.

2. If you do need to reference something, leave a verbal cue such as "[All Caps]Research" or something. Then you don't interrupt your practice.

3. Even if you don't have a blog, maybe this is a way to get into the habit of writing about what it's like to write, in some kind of writer's journal—it may reveal some surprising insights about your process or feelings.

Next step: Dictate 2,500 words in your work in progress.

Dictation Drill 13: Describing a Picture

"Pictures deface walls more often than they decorate them."

— William Wordsworth

Objective: To become more adept at describing a visual image as if speaking conversationally, to become more proficient in describing things without someone present as an audience.

1. Find an interesting picture on the Internet or elsewhere.

2. If you have trouble, pretend you are describing the scene to a friend. Describe the image using the same language you would use conversationally.

3. For an interesting twist, you could also describe this picture as though you are standing in the scene. This would allow you to also express sensory descriptions, such as sight, smell, taste, attach, and sound.

Next step: Dictate 2,500 words in your work in progress.

Dictation Drill 14: Retelling a Story You Have Never Told Aloud

"Don't pass it by—the immediate, the real, the only, the yours."

— Henry James

Objective: To practice being able to think of a story you have just experienced and retell it.

Speak about something that happened that was really important to you, that you've never explained or described aloud.

1. If you get stuck, talk about your day thus far instead.

2. You could also think of a story line you particularly enjoyed reading, watching, or hearing in the past day or so. It could be a published story, movie, television show, or even experience shared by a friend. Just be sure it is a story you have never spoken out loud.

2. Dictate the story as you would to someone who has never experienced it.

3. For another version of this, read a chapter in a book you like then retell it in your own words as if you are the writer. Who knows, you may like your version of your favorite stories even better and boost your ego. An ego is a valuable thing for a writer to have. It helps you be able to keep going rather than self-editing so much!

4. If you need to, jot down plot beats or points to help you remember the story line as you are dictating it.

Next step: Dictate 2,500 words in your work in progress.

Dictation Drill 15: Describing a Scene as It Happens

"Welcome, O life! I go to encounter for the millionth time the reality of experience and to forge in the smithy of my soul the uncreated conscience of my race."

— James Joyce, A Portrait of the Artist as a Young Man

Objective: To become more adept at dictating a scene you observe as it happens, so that it will be easier to describe scenes from your imagination.

Narrate a scene as it happens before you, rather than from your imagination.

1. For this one, don't just use your imagination. Actually go watch people in a public place from a respectful distance. Don't be rude or freak people out!

2. If you don't want to venture forth, watch a favorite DVD or show on mute and describe it like a bystander.

3. Describe the general goings-on or dictate a specific story element: character, setting, mood, and so on. You could try on different points of view from which to view the scene.

4. Bonus points for going where you might get inspiration for your work in progress.

Next step: Dictate 2,500 words in your work in progress.

Dictation Drill 16: Describing Emotional Experience

"Art is not a handicraft, it is the transmission of feeling the artist has experienced."

— Leo Tolstoy

Objective: To become more adept at describing your emotions as they happen, so that it will be easier to describe your characters' emotions from your imagination.

This one's simple in concept but many people don't have much practice at it. So the bonus is, becoming a better communicator not just a better dictationist. Verbalizing, even if just to yourself, can be excellent and affordable therapy!

1. Dictate *your* emotions, not your characters'. Describe your difficult or fabulous emotions as they happen or as they happened earlier in the day.

2. Try to find new ways to describe what you feel, not the same words you typically use.

3. Try making comparisons to other seemingly unrelated things you know about when describing your feelings.

4. If you're neutral, that's an emotion too. Talk about it like you have to describe the phenomena to some sentient being that doesn't have emotions.

Dictation Drill 17: Meditation & Visualization

"There are two ways of seeing: with the body and with the soul. The body's sight can sometimes forget, but the soul remembers forever."

— Alexandre Dumas, The Count of Monte Cristo

Objective: To leverage mental visualization toward actually dictating more fluidly.

I have heard a lot of examples of entertainment-oriented professionals visualizing their performance in order to attain better or more consistent results. Writers can do the same thing with dictation. You're going to visualize what it will be like to dictate like a pro.

1. Don an open mind! You don't have to love visualization but you shouldn't knock it until you try it!

2. Sit or lie down so you can get lost in it. Close your eyes and breathe deeply.

3. Picture yourself sitting, standing, or walking—however you are going to dictate.

4. For at least several minutes, picture yourself going through the motions of dictation steadily and fluidly. Be detailed. Imagine yourself going into the room, sitting down, turning on your computer, and so on or leaving your house and beginning your walk for mobile dictation.

5. The idea is to practice feeling calm about it before you're actually doing it. There are all sorts of things you can do with this:

· Picture yourself overcoming brain fogs

· Picture how it will feel to be on a roll dictating

· Abstractly picture your words filling the screen

That's all there is to this drill. Just picture it, then jump into your work in progress for the day. Notice whether it feels different to have started with visualization.

Next step: Dictate 2,500 words in your work in progress.

Dictation Drill 18: Verbalize Your Favorite Writing Prompts

"I have always had more dread of a pen, a bottle of ink, and a sheet of paper than of a sword or pistol."

— Alexandre Dumas, The Count of Monte Cristo

Objective: To become more adept at dictating creative fiction, by dictating rather than typing or handwriting responses to writing prompts.

The internet is full of writing prompts to help you get started with ideas. Consider simply verbalizing your responses to them.

1. Since this drill starts the section on verbalizing your work in progress, I suggest applying the writing prompt to your plot or characters, even if you are a detailed outliner and it doesn't fit in with your plan. You can always throw it out if it doesn't end up working.

2. Here's an example. If the writing prompts says: ALL I NEEDED TO BE HAPPY, I could start rambling about my villain thinking about the one thing she or he needs to be happy and how they plan to make sure they get it.

Today's dictation of your work in progress is a bit different. Still 2,500 words in your work in progress, but stop in the middle of a thought or sentence (read tomorrow's drill if you want to know why).

Dictation Drill 19: Dangling Thought Warm-up

"Perhaps I really regard myself as an intelligent man only because throughout my entire life I've never been able to start or finish anything."

— Fyodor Dostoyevsky, Notes from Underground

Objective: To practice picking up on a scene mid-sentence or mid-thought.

Many writers have adopted the habit of ending writing session and leaving the scene, paragraph, or even sentence unfinished. By leaving one's thoughts and dangling in this way, many writers claim their subconscious is more apt to try to complete it. The idea is that it will help you jump right back in to a previous line of thought of thinking. The idea is to reorient your mind to the previous set session.

This could be a key to making dictation more natural for you.

1. The previous day, leave the scene, paragraph, or sentence unfinished.

2. The next day or session, read the last thing you wrote.

3. Continue dictating from where you left off. Pay attention to how this feels to begin dictating from the middle of a thought rather than having to create brand-new material right off the bat.

Next step: Dictate 2,500 words in your work in progress.

Dictation Drill 20: Multiple Scene Lead-ins Warm-Up

"To express oneself badly is not only faulty as far as the language goes, but does some harm to the soul."

— Socrates

Objective: To practice thinking and speaking a scene from different angles.

Expressing a scene as awesomely as you can often comes down to point of view. You may also find that new points of view help you dictate and create more fluidly. Sometimes this alleviates pressure you never knew was there for you.

Take the same scene and dictate it five different ways. As you notice which ones resonate with you, keep in mind that the first ones might be harder just because you're warming up—but that's a useful insight, too. Maybe this process unlocks something for you, and you can use it whenever you're getting started with a dictation session.

Here are some options to play with:

· Five different times of day: morning, noon, afternoon, dusk, midnight

· Five different character POVs

· Five different motivations your character has for doing something

· Five different ways your character could get hurt

Next step: Dictate 2,500 words in your work in progress.

Dictation Drill 21: Author Interview Role Play

"Besides, nowadays, almost all capable people are terribly afraid of being ridiculous, and are miserable because of it."

— *Fyodor Dostoyevsky, The Brothers Karamazov*

Objective: To become more adept at thinking on your feet by describing the major elements of your story.

Practice talking about your novel while also refining on your story's main points. Have this recorded or dictate it as you would the other drills so you have a reference document to look over before conventions and such.

1. Have a friend actually interview you about your book.

2. Watch author interviews if you have some time to see how they respond and scribble down the questions they were asked.

3. If it's not working, take on a different persona. Imitate authors' manner of speaking to find your own voice.

Next step: Dictate 2,500 words in your work in progress.

218 | THE PRODUCTIVE AUTHOR'S GUIDE TO DICTATION

Dictation Drill 22: Vocalizing Character Voices

"If so many men, so many minds, certainly so many hearts, so many kinds of love."

— Leo Tolstoy

Objective: To play with adding more depth to conversations by trying subtly unique voices for each character in your story.

Dickens reportedly created voices for his characters, which he acted out in front of mirror. If you want to be as cool as this, dictate a new scene with *subtly* different voices. Remember that dictation software operates off a voice profile, so getting too far from the norm can work against you.

1. Think of a new scene with a couple characters and imagine a voice for each.

2. This is a great way to make dictation more fun and entertaining, but it also carries the advantage of making your story's dialogue really come to life.

Next step: Dictate 2,500 words in your work in progress.

Dictation Drill 23: Narrating to a Soundtrack

"Such sweet compulsion doth in music lie."

— John Milton

Objective: To become more adept at narrating a scene while listening to music or a soundtrack.

I have created audio soundtracks for my novels for some time but I only recently clued in to using music *while* dictating. Ear buds, hello!

1. Think of an upcoming scene and a song that would be great for it if it was in a movie or something.

2. Put an ear bud in and start playing the track. Then start dictating the scene like you normally would.

3. This simultaneous approach may not work for you. Instead, you could listen to a soundtrack for a scene before dictating it.

4. I use this trick even while walking. I put one ear bud in my ear while leaving the other ear free, then I dictate into my digital recorder or iPhone using the free Dragon mobile app. It's vastly entertaining.

Next step: Dictate 2,500 words in your work in progress.

Dictation Drill 24: Describing Sensory Experience

"I used to imagine adventures for myself, I invented a life, so that I could at least exist somehow."

— Fyodor Dostoyevsky

Objective: To become more adept at describing sensory experiences from your imagination.

Describe what the mood of an upcoming scene in your work in progress feels, tastes, smells, and sounds like.

1. Even if you don't use any of this it gets you into a visceral state from which to write or dictate the scene.

2. If this is difficult, describe the same sensory experiences of an upcoming event in your own real life, but then come back to this imaginative version.

Next step: Dictate 2,500 words in your work in progress.

Dictation Drill 25: Dictating from Your Novel-Planning Materials

"The only obligation to which in advance we may hold a novel, without incurring the accusation of being arbitrary, is that it be interesting."

— Henry James

Objective: To leverage your novel-planning devices toward dictating scenes.

You likely have some written or visual guides and inspirations for your story. You can reference those while you dictate.

1. Not every writer uses an outline, but a lot of us do and I recommend it. If you have one, looking at it for story beats can help you move your dictation along more fluidly. If you don't already have a novel, scene, or chapter outline, consider writing one down—even a very simple one.

"Order is the key to all problems." — Alexandre Dumas, The Count of Monte Cristo

2. Many writers create a binder, often referred to as a Bible, for their fictional worlds and characters. This can be a powerful tool for dictating fiction, because it anchors your creativity in the setting of your story. In my experience, visual cues help me get through moments of dictation writers block.

"It takes a great deal of history to produce a little literature." — Henry James

3. As you dictate a new scene, practice referring to these planning materials simultaneously. This is another one of those trial and error things. You may find you are completely bothered by that kind of multi-tasking, but chances are you can use your outline to get traction on where your dictation needs to go.

Next step: Dictate 2,500 words in your work in progress.

Dictation Drill 26: Dictating from Vocabulary Word Prompts

"Mastery of language affords one remarkable opportunities."

— Alexandre Dumas

Objective: To become more fluid at dictation by using a bank of vocabulary words to keep creative momentum up.

I have learned that when my dictation became choppy, I can glance at a sheet of random vocabulary words to spur me on. For example, I might see the word 'stratosphere' and my mind can wrap a creative idea or description around that as an anchor for all sorts of new ideas.

1. Create vocabulary prompts on a sheet of paper. I create a bank of these on a chalkboard every week, so I can draw from them during dictation.

2. Begin dictating a new scene in your work in progress and when you find yourself stalling, glance at the words without forcing it. The idea here is to be non-judgmental, like in stream of consciousness writing or brainstorming.

Next step: Dictate 2,500 words in your work in progress.

10 Tips for Dictating Email

Even if you don't use office software programs, you likely use email. What if you could write messages with your voice rather than doing all that typing?

Here are my top tips for using email clients installed on your computer or device, like Outlook, or popular webmail accounts like Gmail.

1. If you haven't already, be sure to setup or assign your device's default mail service. This varies by operating system.

2. To check your inbox throughout the day, simply say [Check for New Email].

3. Use simple email commands. Examples: [Open Mail], [Close Mail], [New Mail], [Delete Mail], [Forward This] / [Forward Mail], [Reply to This] / [Reply to Mail].

4. Use commands for Microsoft Outlook without Outlook being active.

5. Use Dragon Voice Shortcuts to individual contact members. Examples: [Create Message], [Send email to Francesca Wilson], [Book Meeting with Nick Silas and Brodie Taylor], etc.

6. Use Dragon Voice Shortcuts in reference to a topic. Examples: [Create Mail About Cat Food], [Create Task About Yoga Class].

7. If you are using Gmail, it may help to opt for Basic HTML display (versus Standard).

8. Navigate among messages and tasks using directional commands to specify the number of arrow motions. Examples: [Move Up 4], [Move Down 1], etc.

9. Consider applying the Increase Accuracy From E-mail feature, which gives Dragon permission to assimilate vocabulary in your sent email. This can improve accuracy, particularly with tricky company jargon or people's names you interact with often.

10. Also consider adding e-mail addresses, contact names, and other information you are likely to dictate often to settings such as Vocabulary or Spoken Forms.

10 Tips for Dictating Social Media

You can post status updates to Facebook and Twitter using Dragon dictation.

Here are my top tips for jumping into this:

1. An active Facebook or Twitter account is of course required and you will need to authorize this functionality the first time you do it.

2. You can only use Dragon with one Facebook and one Twitter account at a time.

3. Facebook and Twitter do not even need to be open for the post updates to go through.

4. Use the [Post that to Facebook] or [Post that to Twitter] command to use something you just said as your status update.

5. To dictate your post, say [Post to Facebook] [Just making homemade apple cider, no big deal!] or [Post to Twitter] [Just tweeting this using Dragon dictation, no big deal!].

6. While you can post something you just dictated (such as text in Word or Outlook), you cannot post something from a web page or PDF.

7. If you wax eloquent you can use the [Next Line] command for separation of paragraphs. But you probably won't get too eloquent because:

8. Posting this way is subject to a 120-character limit for Twitter and a 420-character limit for Facebook.

9. Dragon lists this warning in its help documentation: Facebook and Twitter both use spam filters that restrict the number of posts, and if you exceed the limit for a given time period your account on the site is locked out for 24 hours. Spam limits are not documented for security reasons.

10. If you are worried you might accidentally send a post to social media without meaning to, you can deactivate these commands altogether via More Commands.

10 Tips for Dictating a Word Processing Document

Word processing through dictation is easier in some programs than others. I suggest Microsoft Word to dictate a well-formatted document.

Here are my top 10 tools for creating more structure and pizazz:

1. To get to know which commands work in your word processor, activate Dragon and open the word processor, then ask [What Can I Say?]".

2. Also find tips specific to your word processor by searching Dragon's Help Topics from within the program. I found sections for Microsoft Word (including Word Online), Google Docs, Corel WordPerfect, and OpenOffice.

3. For Microsoft Word to work with Dragon, you may need to enable the COM Word Add-in for Dragon dictation

4. Use Dragon's Document List to add documents or folders of many documents you would like Dragon to learn new words from. Awesome! I did this with my WIP (work in progress) so Dragon would recognize names and such more accurately.

5. Get acquainted with the several Recognition Modes on the right end of the Dragon Bar. In addition to the default Normal Mode for commands and text, you can have Dragon focus on one or the other with Command Mode or Dictation Mode. Also check out Number Mode and Spell Mode if Dragon just isn't recognizing something you want it to.

6. You can adjust the pause duration required before Dragon recognizes commands by selecting Options – Commands. Review other options here while you are at it.

7. Margin Commands. For example, in Dragon, say [Fit Left Margin to 1], [Fit Right Margin to Point 5], [Fit Top Margin to 1], or [Fit Bottom Margin to 2].

8. Zoom Commands. For example, in Dragon say [Zoom to 25 Percent].

9. Your accuracy may benefit from updating your User Profile, which you can search for from within Dragon.

10. Remember, you can be a hybrid dictator. Using dictation for every move in a word processing program may not be the most efficient way to create a document. Fit the tool to the task.

10 Tips for Dictating a Spreadsheet

Do writers use spreadsheets? I know I do. Spreadsheets are my outlining tool of choice, for example.

Here are my top 10 tips for dictating a spreadsheet with Dragon.

1. Programs such as Microsoft Excel do not have full text controls in Dragon, so a Dictation Box pops up. Dictate your words in here and they will be transferred to various text fields in your presentation document.

2. Navigate cells in a variety of ways, using [Next Row], [Previous Row], [Next Column], or [Previous Column] commands. You may also be interested in [Move to Cell] commands and [Move Up], [Move Down], [Move Right], or [Move Left] commands. Examples: [Move to Cell C9], [Move Up 2], [Move Right 4], etc.

3. You can also simply select or highlight rows or columns by stating their name. Example: [Row 10] or [Column E].

4. This is a little kooky, but for advanced columns with more than one letter in the name (CD), you must use the alpha-bravo form. Example: [Charlie Daniel] or [Move to Charlie Daniel].

5. Use the hide or unhide row or column commands to focus in on information. Example (may need to select range first): [Hide Row] or [Unhide Column].

6. Sort by selecting the range then saying the [Sort the Selection] command.

7. After moving to a cell, populate it with commonly-used equations like sum or average by using directional commands. Examples: [Sum the Values on the Right];

[Average the Values on the Left]; [Sum the Values Above]; [Average the Values Below].

8. Use AutoFill, which completes a pattern to a designated range of cells using the [Fill This Cell] command. Example: [Fill This Cell Up (or Down) 4], [Fill This Cell Left (or Right) 10], etc.

9. Change the numerical formatting of a selected cell or range, by speaking the [Set This To] command. Example: [Set This Cell to Fractions in Tenths]; [Set This Row to Decimals in Hundredths]; etc.

10. Remember, you can be a hybrid dictator. Using dictation for every move in a spreadsheet program may not be the most efficient way to create a spreadsheet. Fit the tool to the task.

10 Tips for Dictating a Slide Show Presentation

Authors find opportunities to create and present slide show presentations from programs such as Microsoft PowerPoint. You can dictate these as well!

Here are my basic tips for dictating a slide show presentation:

1. Presentation programs such as Microsoft PowerPoint do not have full text controls in Dragon, so a Dictation Box pops up. Dictate your words in here and they will be transferred to various text fields in your presentation document.

2. Start a new presentation by saying [Open New Presentation] but in my experience, this command only worked some of the time so I don't mess with it.

3. Format words by saying [Select All], then [Set Font to (Font Name) or (Font Size)]. Example: [Select All] then [Set Font to Times New Roman 12].

4. This is a bit goopy but you can use the MouseGrid Window to select different fields. Example: [MouseGrid Window] then position the mouse point over a text field followed by [Mouse Click].

5. To switch to another slide use the [View Slide] command. Example: [View Slide 4].

6. To present a slide show use these commands: [Begin the Slide Show], [Press Enter] to advances the slide.

7. Exit the slide show by saying [Escape].

8. Just like in Word, you can change text to bullets by voice selecting some text and saying [Bulletize That].

9. Hide or show the ruler by saying [Toggle the Ruler Off (or On)].

10. Remember, you can be a hybrid dictator. Using dictation for every move in a program may not be the most efficient way to create a presentation. Fit the tool to the task.

10 Tips for Dictating Notes

Much of researching your novel likely involves taking notes—and there are ways or there are ways. If you don't use note-taking software, your current system might work fine for you but many people end up finding more utility by taking advantage of desktop and mobile digital note-taking software like Microsoft OneNote, Evernote, and Google Keep.

Here are my tips for dictating with note-taking software:

1. Microsoft OneNote, Evernote, and Google Keep do not have as many commands programmed into Dragon, but you can still do basic dictation in them thanks to the Dictation Box.

2. Keep it simple. Use notes as prompts not the actual draft, in my opinion.

3. Use it like a word processor. You can also do full-fledged excerpts if that's how you work best, however. For that, you'll want the desktop version of Microsoft OneNote.

4. Keep an eye on your screen. Connectivity issues may delay your transcribed text.

5. Consider going beyond the cheapest option. Note programs such as Evernote offer more at higher price tiers.

6. Take advantage of IFTTT (If This Then That) and other third-party apps.

7. Integrate web clippers if they are available for your note program.

8. Take advantage of OCR, which creates digital text from pictures.

9. Integrate with Kindle highlights.

10. Remember, you can be a hybrid dictator. Using dictation for every move in a program may not be the most efficient way to create your notes. Fit the tool to the task.

For more detail on how to do these things in programs like Microsoft OneNote, Evernote, and Google Keep, visit my About.com Note-taking Software site.

10 Tips for Dictating Web Searches

Much of researching your novel likely involves the internet, though many other ways are available. Here's how to get dictation involved with that process.

1. You may need to enable Dragon Web Extensions for your browser (Internet Explorer, Google Chrome or Firefox).

2. Set a default search engine if you haven't already, so that you can dictate the [Search the Web] command. Ex: [Search the Web for Sloths in South America].

3. Even with that default set, or if you switch search engines a lot, you can dictate the [Search (search engine) For] command for Yahoo!, AOL, Bing, and Google. Example: [Search Bing for Best Train Rides in Europe].

4. Search content type as well using the [Search (content type) For] command, for news, images/photos/pictures, maps, shops, and video/movies. Example: [Search Images for Iceland].

5. You can state commands or keyboard shortcuts if you are more used to those. Example: In Windows, you can say either [Click Go] or these others: [Press Enter], [Refresh Page], [Press F5], [Open New Tab], or [Press Control T].

6. While you cannot do this for every website yet, you can use the [Search (website)] command for About.com, Amazon, eBay, MSN, Twitter, and Wikipedia. Example: [Search About dot com for Office Software Reviews].

7. You can use the [Open Top Site] command. Example: [Open Top Site for Travel Destinations].

8. Once on a site, you can use the [Click (Link Name)] command. Example: On a site about animals living in cold climates, say [Click About Penguins].

9. Use the [Find on This Page] command to search for words on a site. Example: [Find on This Page Penguins].

10. Select form objects vocally as well using the [Click (Object Type)] command. Example: [Click Checkbox], [Click Radio Button], or [Click Text Field].

What to Do If You Want More Practice

Here are some great ways to get more practice, in addition to continuing on your work in progress:

1. Repeat drills in this book.

2. More stream of consciousness! I do this just about every day.

3. Repeat exercises and practice excerpts.

4. Find more excerpts at www.gutenberg.com. You can create prompts like I did by using Find and Replace ex: (Find: ! then Replace with [Exclamation Mark], for example).

5. Create your own practice excerpts from literature you love.

6. Dictate another novel! No matter how slow, and knowing you will get faster.

What To Do If The Whole Thing Is Just Too Frustrating

"We lost because we told ourselves we lost."

— Leo Tolstoy

I went through this feeling, too. Here are my suggestions, because it really is worth it to gain this skill. Above all, keep in mind you are probably making more progress than you think.

1. **Give it a month.** With so many options, you owe it to yourself. In my experience, I was clunking along until one day all that hidden progress found its zenith and I was dictating with wild abandon. Maybe it will be that way for you.

2. **Give it a year.** Do less study time for longer. If you can barely stand dictation but are drawn to the benefits, just do five or ten minutes a day, for many days.

3. **Try intervals or sprints.** It works for workouts, so why not this? Maybe start with dictating for five minutes, get up and take a break, then sprint again. Keep building up.

4. **Leave notes and move on.** Leave yourself research cues rather than pausing for the right word or reference. With dictation, I suggest the spew-then-polish method.

5. **Work on multiple projects.** Try dictating different works, not the same works. In your typing life, you may write all one work in a day but many writers like to work on more than one narrative at a time. Even if you type one way, maybe for some reason you dictate according to another pattern. I found that I like to dictate a new

random story every morning. Then I get into my larger work.

6. **Remove the pressure.** Try dictating something totally secondary in priority. Your laundry list. Your frustrations. Your description of the dreams you dream at night. Your emails. Your social media statuses. Anything. Then come back to fiction or your other main work and try again. Spend some time just dictating your mobile tasks like making calls or accessing text and email messages.

7. **Change locations**. Again, mixing it up can do wonders.

8. **Partner up.** Maybe incorporate this into writers' groups or other social occurrences.

9. **Reward yourself!** For sticking with it, of course.

10. **Be a hybrid dictationist.** Remind yourself that dictation is not the boss of you. Just add a few tricks here and there, while still using the keyboard and mouse. This is actually what most dictation gurus do. No one says it has to be all one or the other.

Hopefully reading and applying the ideas in this guide has been an interesting experience for you, whether you decide dictation is for you or not.

Please consider leaving your review on Goodreads and Amazon.

Find direct links at TheProductiveAuthor.com/Books

"Don't pass it by—the immediate, the real, the only, the yours."

— Henry James

Connect With Us on Social Media

Join our communities and get connected to all the deals and goings-on!

THE PRODUCTIVE AUTHOR:

Twitter:

http://www.twitter.com/ProductiveAuth

Facebook:

http://www.facebook.com/TheProductiveAuthor

Instagram:

http://www.instagram.com/TheProductiveAuthor

Pinterest:

http://www.pinterest.com/ProductiveAuth

AUTHOR CINDY GRIGG:

Google+:

https://plus.google.com/+CindyGrigg/

Twitter:

https://twitter.com/Cindy_Grigg

Facebook:

https://www.facebook.com/authorcindygrigg

Goodreads:

http://www.goodreads.com/user/show/19382357-cindy

Instagram:

http://www.instagram.com/cindygrigg

LinkedIn:

http://www.linkedin.com/pub/cindy-grigg/56/4ba/7a9

Pinterest:

http://www.pinterest.com/CindyGrigg

THE PRODUCTIVE AUTHOR'S GUIDE TO WRITING

Series

Ready for more ideas?

The Productive Author is an imprint for non-fiction guide books within Misch Masch Publishing. Works include other books in the *The Productive Author's Guide to Writing* series.

Each title is focused on timeless writing principles as applied to practical technology tools.

Find other titles by visiting TheProductiveAuthor.com.

Made in the USA
Middletown, DE
31 July 2018